92.0
312.00 CP.
3.391

208. semester hrs
168
60

61.33
42.
NextSem 15

436
3.68

118.33

Debbie
678-0904

Manufacturing Analysis for Productivity and Quality/Cost Enhancement

Second Edition

Manufacturing Analysis for Productivity and Quality/Cost Enhancement

Norbert L. Enrick
Professor, Graduate School of Management
Kent State University

with the collaboration of
Harry E. Mottley, Jr.
Formerly Director of Corporate Reliability
General Instrument Corporation

INDUSTRIAL PRESS, INC.
200 Madison Avenue
New York, New York 10157

Library of Congress Cataloging in Publication Data

Enrick, Norbert Lloyd, 1920-
    Manufacturing analysis for productivity and quality/
cost enhancement.

    Rev. ed. of: Manufacturing improvement through
experimentation. 1968.
    1. Experimental design. 2. Quality control.
3. Mathematical statistics. I. Mottley, Harry E.
II. Title.
T57.37.E57 1982   658.5'6   82-11827
ISBN 0-8311-1146-1

FIRST PRINTING

MANUFACTURING ANALYSIS FOR PRODUCTIVITY AND QUALITY/COST ENHANCEMENT, SECOND EDITION

Preface

The purpose of this volume is to provide a practical guide to the design and analysis of in-plant experiments. Such experiments may have many objectives, either singly or in combination. Among them are the following:

1. Studies to improve product quality and reliability or to enhance the quality/cost ratio.

2. Investigations aimed at analyzing and implementing processing and other manufacturing conditions to enhance productivity -- the output of product in relation to the input of manhours, materials, and energy.

3. Evaluations designed to better understand those factors that contribute to cost, with a view to effective cost reductions.

4. Research for the purpose of better insights regarding facets of training, supervision, and employee participation, so that improvements relating to morale, working conditions, and cooperation can be achieved.

Experiments may be run on the production floor, in the pilot plant, at the research-and-development stage in the laboratory, or in the field. The search is for those methods, materials, and designs that will yield the ultimate, in terms of the current state of the art, in terms of quality, materials utilization, costs, and productivity. The design and analysis methods presented here are applicable to all these areas, but emphasis is placed on examples and illustrations coming from in-plant experimentation.

Questions requiring answers in manufacturing abound for those who view products, processes, methods, and equipment with an alert mind. For example

1. Several oxide additives are being considered for a cutting tool alloy. Which of these additives will serve best in terms of minimal tool wear and cratering?

2. A new process for an electronic component, using new product designs and manufacturing methods, is under study. How much more reliable will be the output; and how are costs, productivity, and marketability affected?

3. How does a new finishing spray compare against others in terms of smoothness of application, product appeal, weathering resistance and wear?

4. How effective and error-proof is a new automatic gage as regards product inspection and rejection of off-quality pieces?

5. Is a new, experimental gasket material really reducing pump leakage incidence in the field?

6. Can the claimed advantages of a new training method be verified in terms of time-to-learn, accomplishments achieved, and performance during actual production situations?

7. Which of several proposed, energy-saving kiln cycles will come closest to maintaining requisite strength characteristics of ceramic insulators?

These types of investigations have the primary purpose of comparisons leading to identification of the best methods, equipment, or materials. Another type of experimentation is designed primarily to establish relationships among a number of variables, as noted below:

1. A nondestructive testing instrument, using a principle of indirect measurement of density, has been developed. How do the readings from this new approach correlate with the results from direct tests? Can the agreement of new vs old method be considered good enough to permit switching?

2. A large amount of scrap and rework have been noted for a machining operation. To what extent will quality improve in response to various levels of cutting speeds? At what point will the cost savings in scrap be best matched with the costs of production in terms of feeds and speeds?

3. What is the relation of steaming time and temperature to the strength of precast concrete beams? How do time and temperature interact and at what point are costs best balanced?

4. How will various amounts of elongation and resilience of a plastic tow cable affect its service life and reliability? What is the best combination?

Other instances involve the need to understand likely consumer reaction to new products or design. The customers may be the mass of individual purchasers or other manufacturers. Market research may then involve the following:

1. Several tentative designs have been developed for a new appliance. Pilot models are taken into the field in an effort to evaluate user preferences. Based on the sampling results achieved, a decision must now be made to freeze on those designs likely to be most successful. It is in the nature of mass manufacture that designs cannot be readily changed once dies have been cut, equipment set up, and processes put into motion.

2. A limited number of color combinations of a product line is all that can be produced economically for next season's marketing. Which of these will best meet demand? Clues obtained from a survey of chain, department, and mail-order

house buyers now require statistical analysis.

3. A series of new types of fasteners is on the drawing board. These are specifically designed for low-cost assembly. Which of these designs promise the most trouble-free operation in long-range production operations at assemblers' plants? A sampling survey must be designed to develop the necessary, analyzable information.

Areas in manufacturing and marketing where systematic analysis can lead to greater productivity and profitability abound in every organization. It takes an inquisitive mind and a forward looking attitude, beginning with top management and perfusing the entire personnel of the company, to maximize the potential benefits. Most of all it should be clear that experimentation can never be left to haphazard arrangement. Here, as in most other instances, good planning is essential. Once an area has been pinpointed in which further knowledge may yield improvements, a systematic procedure may follow these steps:

1. State the information sought, including the types of experimental runs needed, test procedures to be followed, and comparative costs of performing the experiment. Document the potential gains.

2. Run the experiment, including checks and controls to ensure proper setups, methods, and tests.

3. Analyze the results obtained in terms of their statistical and economic significance.

4. Report the results, highlighting the principal findings and conclusions, and submitting recommendations for translating potential benefits into realization.

Where systematic experimentation is not practiced, there is considerable evidence to suggest that faulty, biased, and misleading work outweighs, at least in number and frequency, the valid accomplishments. Costly decisions, involving the purchase of improper machinery, equipment, or materials, or the adoption of poor designs and processing methods may be the price to be paid simply because crucial precautions were not taken.

In this volume, we shall endeavor to develop the principles and practice of sound experimentation. In a world of human fallibility where the search for knowledge often can go astray, these principles will serve as effective guards against faulty conclusions. The principal means of analyzing the outcomes from a well-planned and executed experiment is the application of statistical techniques. We will demonstrate how to apply these techniques in simple and multi-factor experiments. Particularly, the multi-variate approach to experimentation is what sets modern research apart from and many times above older methods, which could look at only "one variable at a time." With modern methods we can thus with a few days' experimentation understand complex multi-variate relationships that, in earlier times, would have required years. Such is the power of soundly designed, practically

executed, and statistically evaluated experimentation. These new
skills are developed gradually, step-by-step in this book. The reader is
encouraged to participate intensively by doing the case-problems provided continuously as we move from simple to more-sophisticated
applications. A large amount of solid knowledge can thus be covered
in a relatively condensed time.

A not infrequent student plaint is: "Spare me the details of
calculations. Just show me what each method does. I can then do the
work on a computer, using the right program." Actually, however, things
are not that simple. Humans are still needed to make judgments on which
particular techniques may be applicable, on how to deal with special
situations, and on what conclusions and recommendations are warranted
from the analysis work. Before one can choose, use, and interpret
computer programs and output, one requires a thorough knowledge of the
various statistical analysis methods and their applicability to particular research situations. Hence the need to work through illustrative,
often simplified examples that highlight the principles and potential
pitfalls involved.

Only the major essentials of productivity-oriented experiment design and analysis, the ones that are most likely to be needed in practice, will be presented. Once these basics are mastered, applications
involving extended uses or more complex situations can be handled
readily, either by relying on further readings in this field or by obtaining occasional statistical assistance from others.

Contents

Chapter I

PRINCIPLES OF SOUND EXPERIMENTATION

Purpose

The history of industrial development records a few outstanding instances in which a startling new improvement in materials usage, operating method or product design was the outcome of an accidental phenomenon, upon which men with sharp eye and keen mind seized to create a new invention. But such events are very rare. Most discovery is the result of well-planned, carefully performed and competently analyzed experimentation. This applies both to the discovery of some sweeping innovations such as the laser and to the more frequent, mundane but, in total effect, equally important studies -- such as how to reduce the cost of an assembly operation.

Once we have ruled out chance, accident and haphazard procedure as a good source of innovative improvement, we are committed to a systematic approach. When such is used, it has been found that the best designed experiments-- those which tend to give the most reliable and intelligible results-- take cognizance of three essential prerequisites:

1. Balance, so as to give equal weight to the various factors and conditions of the experiment.

2. Randomization within trial conditions of the experiment, so as to avoid potential hidden bias; and

3. Replication, meaning that at least one repeat trial is needed of an experimental trial, so as to be able to evaluate and minimize likely "experimental error."

By themselves, the terms randomization, replication and balance have little immediately recognizable meaning; and in lieu of lengthy theoretical discussion or definitions, it will be preferable to illustrate with examples how these principles are incorporated in practical experiments.

Balancing of Experimental Factors

For a simple case of balancing, examine the sampling inspection of four tote boxes shown in Fig. I-1. The inspector has balanced his sample by randomly selecting the same number of cylindrical parts from each box. The quality of each tote box has thus an equal chance to affect the outcome of the sampling inspection. It is this principle of equal weight that applies to all balancing.

FIGURE I-1. Balancing illustrated from sampling inspection. By randomly selecting an equal number of cylindrical parts from each of the four tote boxes, we have given equal weight to each box, and thus balanced the procedure. Each box -- whether it may turn out to have good or bad quality parts -- has an equal chance to affect the sampling outcome.

For another instance, Fig.I-2 shows two plating compounds, A and B, that are to be evaluated in their effect on the quality of plated parts, produced in two barrels, 1 and 2. It would be improper merely to try Compound A with Barrel 1 and Compound B with Barrel 2, since the two barrels are of different size. Thus, suppose that the parts plated with Compound A turned out to be better than those with Compound B. We could not ascribe the improvement to Compound A, because the barrel size rather than the compound may have been responsible for the result observed.

For proper balance, we must give equal weights to both compounds and barrels. In addition to trying A with 1 and B with 2, we must also try A with 2 and B with 1.

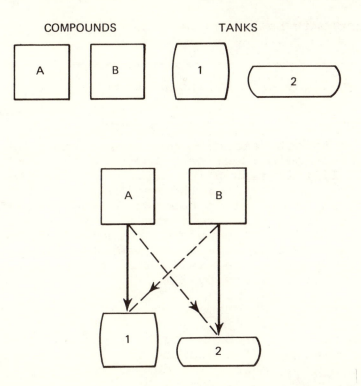

Figure I-2: Two plating compounds, A and B, are to be evaluated in two plating barrels, 1 and 2. It would be improper to merely try A with 1 and B with 2, since the size of each barrel is different, and the plating characteristics — quality, efficiency, etc. — may be as much a function of barrel size as type of compound. Each compound must be tried with each barrel; and, both the combination shown by the solid *and* that shown by the dotted leader lines above must be studied before a valid conclusion, based on a balanced procedure, can be formed.

ASSIGNMENT I-1

Assume that in our plating experiment the two barrels were of identical size. Why might it have still been desirable to balance the experiment?

_____

_____

_____

ASSIGNMENT I-2

Can you give at least two reasons why, despite the desirability of a balanced experiment, you might from a practical standpoint have decided not to balance; viz., test Compound A with Barrel 1 only and B with Barrel 2 only; or else, test Compound B with Barrel 1 only and A with Barrel 2 only?

PRINCIPLES OF SOUND EXPERIMENTATION

1. We might omit balancing because _expensive_

2. Also, we might omit balancing because _time consuming_

Observe that by not balancing you have taken a calculated risk, that because both barrels seem identical, they probably have the identical effects on the plating. If this assumption is correct, then only the compounds will be important. In practice, the engineer may also find it desirable to check such items as condition of bearings, levelness of alignment and other factors on both barrels, so as to guard against undue differences in vibration (worn bearing), partial compound sedimentation (non-level barrel alignment) or other differential actions between the two barrels. Experiments involving faulty equipment can easily lead to erroneous conclusions, and balancing is no complete guard by itself.

Factors and Levels of an Experiment

In order to consider problems of balancing effectively, it is desirable to distinguish between factors and levels in an experiment. The plating example will serve as a vehicle for demonstration:

1. There were two factors. One factor was "type of plating compound," and the other was "plating barrel used."

2. Each of the two factors was held at two levels. The factor "type of plating compound" involved the levels "Compound A" and "Compound B." The factor "plating barrel used" had the two levels "Barrel 1" and "Barrel 2."

In more advanced applications these terms will become especially helpful.

ASSIGNMENT I-3

Assume now what we investigated 3 plating compounds, A, B and C and there were 5 different shaped barrels, 1, 2, 3, 4 and 5. Then, for a fully balanced experiment, indicate the following:

1. Number of factors? _2_

2. Levels of the "plating compound" factor? _3_

3. Levels of the "barrel shapes" factor? _5_

Conditions of an Experiment

A combination of two factor levels is known as a "condition" or "cell." In the original plating problem, there were 4 conditions: A with 1, A with 2, B with 1 and B with 2. These 4 conditions in turn gave each factor and each level equal weight, since they had an equal opportunity to affect the outcome. Hence, the experiment was balanced.

In order to ascertain quickly the number of conditions of a fully balanced experiment, we merely multiply together the number of levels per each factor. Since, in the example just discussed, each of the factors had 2 levels, we state:

Conditions = (Levels of First Factor) x (Levels of Second Factor)

where the first factor is compounds and the second factor is barrel sizes, and therefore:

Conditions = 2 x 2 = 4.

This checks with our actual enumeration of the four conditions, above.

Now as a further example, if the first factor had involved 4 levels and the second factor had had 8 levels, then:

Conditions = 4 x 8 = 32.

While the determination of conditions is simple for few levels, for multifactor experiments involving many levels of each factor it is handy to have the formula shown.

ASSIGNMENT I-4

Assume that the experiment involved 3 plating compounds A, B and C with 5 different shaped barrels. For full balance, how many conditions will one need to run in this experiment?

Conditions = __3__ x __5__ = __15__

Confounding in Experimentation

When experiments are large, it may be impractical, uneconomical and excessively time-consuming to fully balance all factors. When full balance is lacking, some factor effects may be mingled or "confounded" as the experimenter says, and analysis becomes difficult. Yet, we may have no choice but to confound. In such instances, great care must be given to considering the particular conditions that will be omitted in the experiment. At best, confounding involves a carefully weighed compromise as to what information we can afford to sacrifice. In practice, this will often require a great deal of statistical and engineering judgment, since we should strive to confound only those factors that are least likely to exhibit certain effects known as "interaction" (to be discussed later).

PRINCIPLES OF SOUND EXPERIMENTATION

The need for managerial, supervisory, and engineering/scientific personnel to understand the principles and basic procedures of experimental design and analysis is demonstrated over and over again when problems of "confounding" and "interaction" are encountered. Only by close cooperation with the statistician, based on an understanding of the problems and limitations within which his evaluation of experimental test results must proceed, can the best designs be accomplished. Moreover, when the statistician does present the results of his analysis, the degree to which others understand these results will often determine their ability to translate them into worthwhile practical improvements.

Randomization

An illustration of randomization was given in connection with Fig. I-1, in which an inspector was required to select ten pieces from each of four tote boxes. Common sense tells us that he should spread his sample over each box, preferably drawing each piece "blindly" from various parts of the box. Any other procedure is unlikely to give him an unbiased representation in the sample of the contents of the tote box as a whole. For example, let us assume the inspector checked only the first ten pieces from the front and top of each box. An operator who notes such an inspection procedure might be tempted to place his best pieces in that location, with the less perfect ones hidden in other parts of the box.

Aside from willful factors, unknown effects may be operating that make random selection desirable. For example, if there is drift on a machine, then the last pieces produced will not truly represent overall lot quality; or if there is a periodicity in the production process, such as caused by an eccentric drum or other factors that systematically "come and go" during production, then a system sample may happen to synchronize with the periodic variations. To avoid known or unknown bias, randomization in sampling is desirable. The principle of randomization is further illustrated in Figure I-3.

Further Example of Randomization

Four tote boxes, each containing 8 castings, have been obtained from 4 different heat-treating operations. We wish to know the effect of heat-treating on machinability, and we have selected a four-spindle automatic for this operation. Convenience of record keeping would demand that each heat treatment be run on one spindle; such that Treatment A and Spindle 1, Treatment B and Spindle 2, Treatment C and Spindle 3 and Treatment D and Spindle 4 would give the desired trial results.

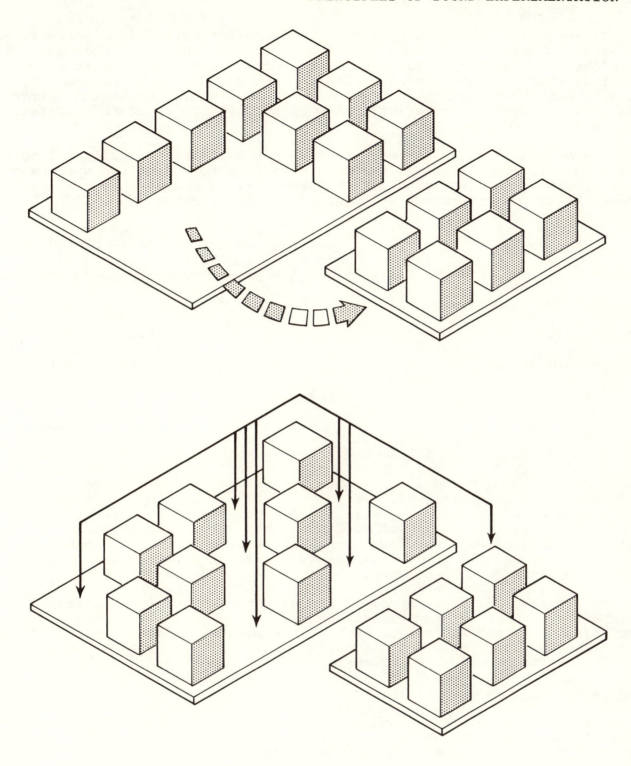

Figure I-3: Principle of randomization. Non-randomness ,in upper sampling (pieces selected from one part of lot) and randomness below (pieces selected from all parts of lot).

We recognize, however, that such an expedient method is also very dangerous. For if there is an unknown deficiency in one of the four spindles, such as a misaligned bearing, worn or dull tool, or loose fitting, then any inferior machining on that spindle might erroneously be ascribed to whatever heat treatment had been run. The best treatment, run on a deficient spindle, will show up poorly. To avoid this pitfall we randomize and balance.

One method is to number each casting per heat treatment, from 1 to 8, and then utilize paper slips numbered similarly to assign two numbers per heat treatment to each spindle. The paper slips, placed in a bowl, are drawn "blindly." One result so obtained is shown below:

	Four Heat Treatments (A to D) and the Eight Casting Numbers per Treatment Assigned to Various Spindles			
	A	B	C	D
Spindle No. 1	2,6	5,4	5,2	4,7
Spindle No. 2	1,4	1,8	6,8	8,1
Spindle No. 3	3,7	2,3	4,7	2,3
Spindle No. 4	8,5	7,6	1,3	6,5

Castings Nos. 2 and 6 from heat treatment A are machined on Spindle No. 1; castings Nos. 1 and 4 from A go on Spindle No. 2 and castings 5 and 4 from B go on Spindle No. 1; etc., until all 8 castings per heat treatment have been assigned, two per spindle and treatment. Assume now that, unknown to the experimenter, Spindle No. 3 is defective. It is bound to affect the quality of machining, but since Spindle No. 3 has randomly received castings from each heat treatment, we may expect that the effect of Spindle No. 3 will be equalized. Thus, in randomizing we have also taken care of balance.

As a further discussion point, let us assume that you also wanted to know at the end of the experiment whether any spindle might have been operating in either a superior or inferior manner. Since the experiment was balanced and randomized, a comparison of the four spindle averages would serve to reveal this information.

Use of Random Numbers Tables

More elegant than the drawing of paper slips, and from certain theoretical consideration also more scientific, is the use of random numbers, as tabulated in the Appendix. For our castings example, we would proceed as follows:

1. Decide on a definite sequence in which to assign random castings to the 16 experimental conditions or cells. (Since there are two factors, heats and spindles, each with 4 levels, there are 4 x 4 = 16 conditions.)

2. For example, you may decide to assign numbers from left to right, for heat treatments A to D, and to assign spindles within each heat treatment from top of column to bottom, thus from spindle 1 down to spindle 4 as in the tabulation in the preceding section. Thus, the first condition to be taken care of is A-1 (spindle 1 for treatment A), then A-2, then A-3, then A-4, next B-1, then B-2, etc., until finally we reach D-4. For each condition, we need 2 numbers.

3. A one-digit number between 1 and 8 is required. We will thus use only the last digit of each random number found in the table. If the number happens to be 0 or 9, ignore it and proceed to the next number.

4. Decide on how you wish to travel through the Random Numbers table. Any method is acceptable, provided you have decided on it before you start using it (blindly, therefore) and not after you have already looked at the numbers. Suppose we decide to travel horizontally on each line. When the numbers in a given line have been used up, we will go to the next lower line, far left-hand entry and continue our travels.

5. Now, closing our eyes, we let our index finger travel over the page. It happens to come at rest on line 10, column 6. Going from left to right, we will now pick up last digits, which are 5, 7, and 4 on this line. The next line, 11, provides us with these digits from columns 1 to 8: 7, 9, 0, 8, 8, 9, 0, 5. We can begin to assign castings.

6. To condition A-1, we will assign the digits 5 and 7, just found. Next, for A-2 we will use digit 4, but we cannot use the next 7, because we have already assigned casting No. 7 to spindle 1. The next two numbers are 9 and 0, which we ignore since there is no casting No. 0 or 9. The next number is 8. Cell A-2 will therefore use casting No. 8, together with the previously assigned No. 4. The remaining open numbers 8, 9, 0, and 5 above are all unsuitable. So, we return to the Random Numbers table, now starting with Line 12, for additional digits.

The process described will yield the desired numbers. While the procedure may seem tedious, the reader should be assured that with a little experience it is actually much faster to use a Random Numbers table than to explain how one applies it. In fact, random numbers can be picked quicker from a table than from the more laborious paper-slip drawing process.

ASSIGNMENT I-5

You are asked to assign random castings to heat-treatments and spindles by continuing the procedure started above.

| | Four Heat Treatments (A to D) and the Eight Casting Numbers per Treatment Assigned to Various Spindles | | | |
	Treatment A	Treatment B	Treatment C	Treatment D
Spindle No. 1	5,7			
Spindle No. 2	4,8			
Spindle No. 3	6,1			
Spindle No. 4	2,3			

The assignment will come out differently from the previous one, since we then used a different method.

ASSIGNMENT I-6

Even though you used a table of random numbers, you will find that all of your colleagues in the course have obtained the same assignment of castings to conditions. How can this be, if we are supposed to do "random" assignments?

_____

_____

Why need you not worry about this phenomenon in actual applications of random numbers usage (that is, even though all students who did the job correctly got the same assignments, this is of no concern so far as the aspects of randomness are concerned?)

_____

_____

Pitfalls in Non-Randomization

Once the balance of experimental factors and factor levels has been assured, samples must be randomly selected within each experimental condition. A case history will serve to underscore the type of embarrassment that may be encountered if randomization is overlooked.

A producer of wire coils for telephone ringers wished to study the effect on quality of a new type of plastic tension disc on his 10-spindle winder. A diagram of his set-up is given in Fig. I-4. Because of a very small diameter wire, it was essential to have high-precision discs that involved a minimum of unwinding friction of the stock from the supply spools. Believing randomization a needless frill, the engineer simply placed four of the new discs on the motor-end side of the winder and compared these against the existing metallic tensions on the bearing-end side. He reported that the plastic tensions gave better coil-winding quality, with more even coil spacing and more uniform electrical resistances. When all winders in the plant had been equipped with the new

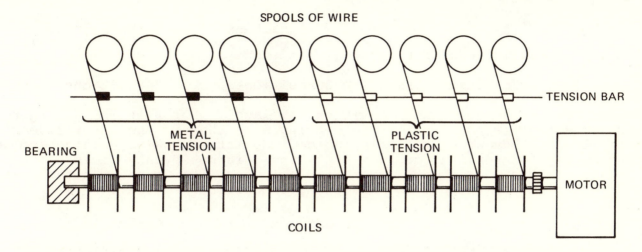

Figure I-4: Schematic of winding experiment. It was desired to investigate the effect of plastic versus metallic tension discs on coil quality. The engineer ignored the precaution to randomize, placing all metallic tensions near the bearing side and all plastic tensions near the motor side of the winder. Because of shaft distortion and some tension-bar misalignment, these machine-effects were then confused with "tension effects."

plastic tensions, based on this recommendation, it was discovered with some dismay that no real quality improvement had resulted.

On checking, the winder used for the experiment was found to have a distorted shaft. This, coupled with a slight misalignment of the tension bar, had unduly harmed the quality of the coils near the bearing end of the winder, where the metallic tensions had been. It was the effect of the distortions and misalignments in the machine, and not the tension posts, that the engineer had observed. Randomized tension post allocation would have minimized these external effects and yielded more correct outcomes.

<u>Pitfalls in Non-Balance</u>

Randomization would have scrambled the two types of tensions (metallic and plastic) among the 10 positions on the winding machine. This procedure would, by itself, also have tended to balance out the biasing effects of the position of tensions with regard to motor or bearing end. Randomizing is a type of balancing, but because it relies on random dispersion it is not as effective as conscious balancing for known effects. For example, if the engineer had realized in advance that position of tensions in relation to motor or bearing end is important, he might have balanced the experiment as follows:

	Bearing Side	Motor Side
Metallic Tension Discs	2 Positions	3 Positions
Plastic Tension Discs	3 Positions	2 Positions

Note that we still have a slight unbalance. For this design, there are more plastic tensions on the bearing side than on the motor side of the winder. But we have little choice. No matter how we arrange it, we can only put 5 tensions on each side, and 5 is not evenly divisible by 2. An alternative would be to ignore two spindles, let us say the farthest on each side, so that we now have only 8 positions to fill:

	Bearing Side	Motor Side
Metallic Tension Discs	2 Positions	2 Positions
Plastic Tension Discs	2 Positions	2 Positions

As a further experimental alternative, we might have maintained the 5 positions per side, but alternated; such as by interchanging metallic and plastic tensions after the experiment has run for half its total planned time.

One constant pitfall in experimentation, is that we may fail to recognize certain factors that call for balancing. However, as long as we resort to randomization we will generally succeed in minimizing the effects of hidden bias.

ASSIGNMENT I-7:

Assume that your experiment has been set up so as to utilize only 8 of the 10 winder positions, half of which are assigned to the metallic and the other half to the plastic tension posts. Recognizing that the winder side may be important, we will elevate it to the status of a factor (in the sense described previously). Therefore, our experiment now has two factors and 2 levels per factor. State these below:

First Factor: _Disc side_ Second Factor: _Disc make-up_

Levels of First Factor: _Bearing; Motor_

Levels of Second Factor: _Metallic; Plastic_

Next, assume that the spindle positions from bearing to motor end of winder are 1, 2, 3, 4, 5, 6, 7, 8, 9, and 10, but that we will not use 1 and 10. Show these spindle positions, by number, as determined by you with the aid of the Random Numbers table (in the Appendix) below:

	Bearing Side		Motor Side	
Metallic Tension Posts:	4	and 3	5	and 9
Plastic Tension Posts:	6	and 7	2	and 8

The result will be a balanced and randomized experimental set-up, for use in conducting the investigation as to whether metallic or plastic tensions will give the best results as regards coil quality.

Replication

Just one single trial is usually not sufficient to permit valid conclusions, just as one swallow proverbially does not make Spring. The universal requirement of quality control and reliability sampling, that a sample must consist of several units, is based on this fundamental truth.

For an experiment to be replicated, it must at least be run twice. The first run and the repeat run together make a replication of two. One further repetition gives a replication of three. Thus "replication" means "number of complete repeats" of the experimental runs. In the instance of the coil-winding experiment, the entire experiment was run only once, so we had no replication. Had we specified another complete run, to be conducted upon completion of the first one, we would have had a replication of two.

Some confusion arises occasionally between "number of determinations" and "number of replications." Referring to the 8-position experiment on the winder, the reader might point to the fact that two positions were used in each experimental condition. Therefore, he might say (erroneously) that the replication was two. Actually, however, all of the posts were run simultaneously, and thus we merely had two repeat determinations per condition. For replication, the entire experiment needs re-running fully.

In some instances, the distinction between number of determinations and replications is not fully ascertainable and may be a matter of opinion. Moreover, practical limitations under the exigencies of actual shop conditions may occasionally make it impossible to replicate. But the risks involved should be understood.

Experimental Error

The great value of replication in both quality control and experimentation is that it provides an estimate of "experimental error." With "error" we do not mean mistakes in running experiments. Instead, we refer to the fact that in any test, some fluctuations or variations are likely to occur. These fluctuations, when they are of a nature that cannot be readily traced to a specific cause, are of the kind that we call "error." Although special tests may be designed seeking to pinpoint most causes of variation, in a particular experiment it is impractical to investigate more than a few of them. It can only be anticipated that the factors not investigated will balance out in a random manner. A certain amount of variability, whose origin it is not feasible or practical to trace, will generally remain. This variability, representing chance causes, is the "experimental error."

The principle of replication is further illustrated in schematic form in Figure I-5. Numerical procedures for evaluating experimental error in quantitative terms will be presented later.

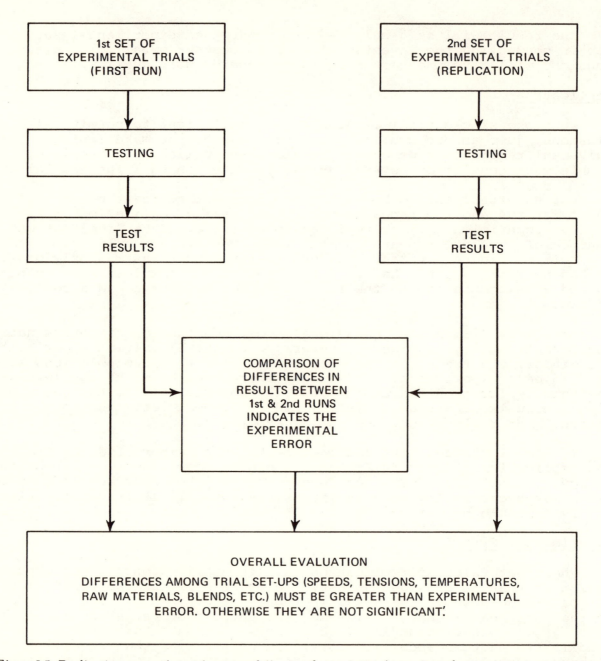

Figure I-5: Replication means that at least two full sets of experimental runs (speeds, tensions, temperatures, materials, blends, admixtures, etc.,) are made.

Sometimes people will feel that with sufficient care, they can be so precise in their work as to eliminate all uncontrolled variations. But in practice they may be mistaken. For example, a chemist who takes undue pains to be "absolutely exact" in weighing his ingredients, may be taking excessive time in his endeavor, thus giving his sample a chance to pick up unwanted moisture from the air.

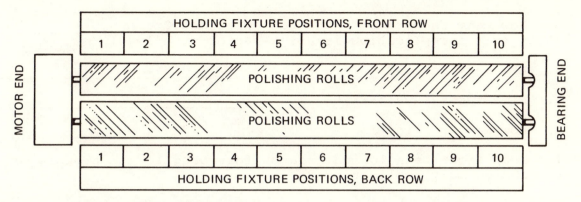

Figure I-6: Auto-polisher. Machine consists of front and back row rolls with corresponding fixtures for positioning of metal blanks to be polished.

ASSIGNMENT I-8

Brightness of metal blanks, achieved by two polishing compounds, A and B, is to be investigated on the automatic polisher in Figure I-6. Although each roll (front and back) serves to polish 10 distinct blanks, only one compound can be put on a roll at a time. It has been decided to make 6 replications, but in each run the compounds on the two rolls should not be the same. When the front roll is on A, for example, the back roll is to be on B.

1. Use a random-numbers table to decide whether on the first run for the front roll you should use compound A or B. This method will permit an unbiased choice. (Hint: Since you must convert numbers to letters, you might define digits 0, 1, 2, 3 or 4 as A, while digits 5, 6, 7, 8 and 9 become B.) Use A__✔__or B____first? (Check one.)

2. Now complete the experimental design below, noting that we decided on unlike compounds for the two rolls on any run. Also, each successive run is to start opposite to the prior one. Thus, if run 1 started with A on the front roll, run 2 will use B on the front roll.

Run No.	Front Roll	Back Roll
1	A	B
2	B	A
3	A	B
4	B	A
5	A	B
6	B	A

3. How many factors were in this experiment? _____1_____
(Note that a replication is not a factor or a level)

4. How many levels?_____2_____

5. Name these levels: _____A & B_____

6. How many replications?_____6_____

7. What might be a logical reason for going to the trouble of running so many replications?

_____

_____

_____

_____

A good experimenter will keep track of the position on which each blank was polished. Then, if he notes a trend in quality from the blanks near the motor end to those near the bearing end, this might indicate a shaft distortion or that bearing wear is present. Other trends may reflect unevenness of roll diameter or differential roll texture conditions.

Also, just because a roll can accept only one compound at a time does not mean that we will never find it desirable to balance the holding fixture positions between motor and bearing-end sides. For example, some other experiment might be concerned with the effect of different pre-treatments of blanks prior to polishing, and the blanks should then be assigned in a balanced-randomized manner to the ten fixture positions per row.

ASSIGNMENT I-9:

State briefly the purpose of the following principles of experimental design:

1. Balance: _____equal weight_____

2. Replication: _____minimizing effects of external effects_____

3. Randomization: _____avoid hidden bias_____

ASSIGNMENT I-10, Review Problem:

A steel mill ships tin plate to two canning plants, who have specified that tin coating shall be at least 0.8 grams per square yard. Recently, the mill and the plants have disagreed with regard to the measured determinations of coating thickness. An experiment is to be conducted to determine whether the mill laboratory, M, and the two plant laboratories, A and B, are performing consistent tests of coating. Important factors to be considered in planning the experiment are:

1. It is impossible to have the identical specimens (discs of tin plate) tested by each laboratory, since measurement of the coating involves the chemical stripping of the tin from the base metal (destructive testing).

2. It is possible to send several closely adjoining discs, taken from a sheet, to the various laboratories in the hope that any differences in tin coating among the discs will "average out." The success of this method depends on how small these differences will be and how many discs are tested per laboratory. If, in fact, the coating-difference effect can be "balanced out" or "averaged out," then any differences in test results that remain will be due to:

   (a) Systematic effects of differences in the measuring technique among the 3 laboratories or other systematic differences and,

   (b) Random variability (experimental error).

3. We must determine how many discs to send to each laboratory and how to select the discs from the sheet. Let us assume that through appropriate studies it has been found desirable that each of the 3 laboratories is to receive 9 discs.

4. A sheet of tin plate, sufficiently long and wide to allow the cutting of 27 discs must be utilized. But, although we believe this sheet to be very uniform throughout, it is possible that there are differences in coating because:

   (a) Some sort of pattern of variation in coating may occur either along the length of width, or both, of the sheet.

   (b) Variations so observed may be produced by many factors, such as electrode positions, "waviness" effects of electrolytic deposition, "edge" effects in processing or patterning in the base metal.

Assume that the tin sheet has been cut as shown below, yielding 9 disc per strip:

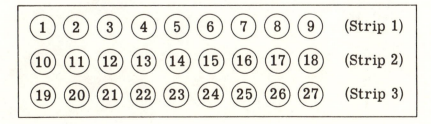

Each circle represents one disc, and the numbers show the sequence in which the discs were obtained by means of a cutting die. Thus, Strip 1 was cut before Strip 2, and Strip 2 before Strip 3.

Next, recalling the problems outlined above, indicate which discs you would ship to what laboratory to maintain a properly balanced, replicated and randomized experiment.

DISC (By Disc Number) ASSIGNED TO THREE LABORATORIES

Strip No.	Mill Lab.			Lab. A			Lab. B		
1	4	3	5	9	6	7	2	1	8
2	11	10	13	16	18	17	15	14	12
3	__	__	__	__	__	__	__	__	__

With regard to the assignment of discs to laboratories, discuss:

1. In what manner is the experiment "balanced"?

Same # of observations for each condition.

2. In what manner is the experiment "replicated"?

Not replicated — to replicate — get another sheet of metal same numbers (4,3,5) etc.

3. What would have been wrong with simply assigning all discs from Strip 1 to Mill Laboratory, M; all discs from Strip 2 to Plant Laboratory B, and all discs from Strip 3 to Plant Laboratory A?

Would have balance no randomization could be variation width wise

4. Indicate what would have been wrong with assigning discs as follows: The sheet is identified by lengthwise sections 1 to 9, and then alternately the 3 discs from each section are sent to the laboratories as shown below:

Sheet Section	Laboratory Receiving Discs		
	A	B	M
1	X		
2		X	
3			X
4	X		
5		X	

Sheet Section	Laboratory Receiving Discs (Cont.)		
	A	B	M
6			X
7	X		
8		X	
9			X

("X" mark indicates Laboratory receiving the 3 discs per section)

If variation is cyclical (wear + tear)

_____

5. Let us assume that you had made this assignment:

	Laboratory		
Strip	M	A	B
~~1~~ 3	22,25,19	20,23,27	21,26,24
2	16,14,11	17,15,13	10,12,18
~~3~~ 1	6, 1, 2	3, 8, 9	5, 7, 4

Then, answer below:

(a) The number of factors investigated is _*diff variables levels studying*_ *2*

(b) The name(s) of these are _*Lab, Strips*_

_____

(c) The number of levels of each factor is given below (use only as many rows as needed):

Factor _*Strip*_ has _*3*_ levels.

Factor _*labs*_ has _*3*_ levels.

Factor _____ has _____ levels.

Summary

We have discussed the general principles of sound experimentation, and spent a considerable amount of time on questions of balance, randomization and replication. In practice, it should be understood that the problem of proper experimental design in the context of these principles is rarely a simple matter. A worthwhile experiment, expected to yield worthwhile results, must be carefully planned. Factors that required balancing must be considered from both an engineering and a practical viewpoint. The attainment of randomization requires thoughtful study, and the amount of replication involves a weighing of cost and time factors. At best, a practical experiment represents a thoughtful compromise among those designs that seem theoretically optimal and the actual design that we can afford under a given set of realistic circumstances and limiting conditions. Full balance, complete randomization and several replications are our goal. How close we actually come to this objective is often a function of the ingenuity of the experimenters in realistic and efficient planning.

Chapter II

FUNDAMENTALS OF STATISTICAL ANALYSIS OF EXPERIMENTS

Purpose

Squeezing the most information from the outcomes of experiments is primarily a function of good statistical analysis. Equipped with this evaluation, the management, engineering, and production personnel concerned can then translate the experimental outcomes into meaningful interpretations and improvements with regard to materials, products or processes. Management, similarly, must be able to understand these analyses so as to be in a good position to properly support research studies and evaluate the merits of new projects, equipment, materials or other facilities and procedures designed to capitalize on improvements attainable.

Statistical methodology encompasses the acquisition, review and analysis of data, thereby becoming a useful tool wherever the outcomes of experiments -- the data collected from trials and tests -- need study, evaluation and interpretation. For this purpose it is only incidentally concerned with functions of recording and tabulating the data, its more important task being to provide a body of methods and techniques for the study of the behavior of measurements. Such questions as: "How many tests (that is, measurements) will be needed?", and "What is the amount of experimental error?" or "How significant are the effects observed for the various factors under study" cannot be answered otherwise.

One cannot begin to meaningfully interpret the results of experiments without a grasp of certain fundamentals of statistical analysis. From the illustrative case histories of the prior chapter, we have gleaned some of the reasons for this need. Variations in data from experiments occur no matter how carefully and diligently the experiments are performed. Sometimes, variability in test results may be so large as to obscure completely the effects of factors and factor levels and even cause incorrect conclusions to be drawn. Lack of uniformity of raw materials or equipment to which experimental treatments are applied, fluctuations in the environmental conditions of temperature, humidity, air-drafts and vibrations, and variable performance of operators, experimenters and the measuring and testing equipment itself all combine to cause a certain amount of variability. We have lumped these factors, to the extent that they are not individually traceable to a particular causative agent, under the name experimental error. Other terms sometimes found are "uncertainty," "random fluctuation or variation," and "chance fluctuation."

One of the great virtues of statistical analysis is that it provides us with a quantitative figure in the form of an index of the variation representing experimental error. By comparing differences among factor and level averages against this error term, one can evaluate the significance of these differences. Further virtues of the statistical approach -- such as permitting the study of several variables in one experiment and then dissecting the outcoming in terms of the relative effect of each variable -- will also be demonstrated.

Nature of a Measurement Process

Anyone who has ever tried to make repeat measurements "under identical conditions" can testify to the fact that his successive readings will vary to some extent. This is true regardless of whether he is repeatedly measuring a dimension of the same machined part on a sensitive micrometer to ten-thousandths of an inch, or the electrical resistance of a semi-conductor to a comparable resolution, or density of material in terms of nuclear backscatter on a nuclear gage particle counter. In fact, if such variation in what appears to be an irregular or random manner, defying prediction but yet falling within certain expected limits, is absent, then this usually and quite defensibly is considered evidence of inadequate accuracy and precision of measurement. The limits noted can be calculated in the form of "control limits" familiar from quality control applications. They define the hopefully narrow domain within which we must expect "experimental error" to reign. Limitations of men, methods, materials and measuring equipment cause this lack of "exact sameness" from test to test under supposedly identical conditions.

The throwing of dice is a prime example of a certain non-repeatability in successive processes. Even though the same die is used successively by the same person on the same table, outcomes will vary randomly. Why? Because the hand imparts on the die a different amount of force each time; its height and angle to the table will vary from throw to throw; and the location of the die within the hand will differ for each instance. Despite this randomness, certain stabilities of outcomes will be apparent from a true pair of dice. Such values as "seven" will appear far more often than a "two" or a "twelve." In fact, if such a pattern does not result from repeated tosses, then the trueness of the dice or the honesty of the thrower will be suspect. In any group of 36 tosses, we may hardly anticipate to duplicate the theoretical prediction of Figure II-1. A certain amount of deviation -- "experimental error" -- is expected, but as we average the outcomes from several sets of 36 tosses, we can rightly anticipate that a fair set of dice tossed honestly will approach relatively closely the theoretical pattern given.

Norman Curve

The distribution of dice throws is a forerunner of the bell-shaped Normal Curve. Conceptually, if we had taken an infinite number of dice and averaged the results of an infinite number of tosses, we would obtain this curve, Figure II-2, which is also typical of the distribution of results from most measurement processes.

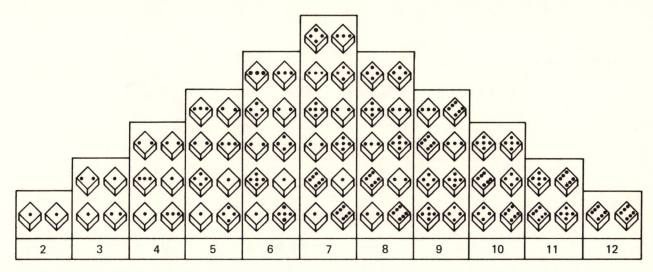

Figure II-1: Dice-throws distribution. This diagram illustrates an application of the probability law to 36 throws of a pair of dice. Normally, these throws will produce the type of distribution pattern shown here, where the combinations "2" and "12" will appear only once for each six times that the combination "7" appears. Where the basic distribution of data in industrial testing and experimentation approximates this type of pattern, mathematical probability laws may be called in to interpret the data. Source: Enrick, N.L. Quality Control & Reliability, 7th ed., 1977, Industrial Press, New York, N.Y. 10157.

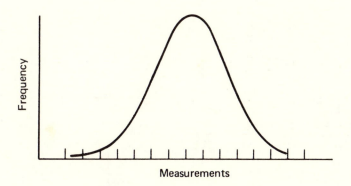

Figure II-2: Normal Curve.

The particular plot is of the form known as a "frequency distribution." The higher the curve is at any point of measurement, the greater is the frequency of occurrence of that value.

An application of the normal curve to the measurement of a production lot is given in Figure II-3. The particular characteristic tested is "yarn size," a measurement of density, evaluated for various bobbins.

FUNDAMENTALS OF STATISTICAL ANALYSIS OF EXPERIMENTS

(Example of Yarn Bobbins)

GIVEN: Average Size, $\overline{X}$ = 50
         Coefficient of Variation, V, = 3%
         Std. Deviation, $\sigma = \overline{X}$ x V = 50 x 3% = 1.5

THEN: from the statistical characteristics of the "normal curve,"
         we may expect approximately that:

         68% of all bobbins will size within 50 ± 1σ = 50 ± 1.5

         95% of all bobbins will size within 50 ± 2σ = 50 ± 3.0

         100% of all bobbins will size within 50 ± 3σ = 50 ± 4.5

GRAPHICAL ILLUSTRATION:

   Percent of Bobbins Falling in Each Group

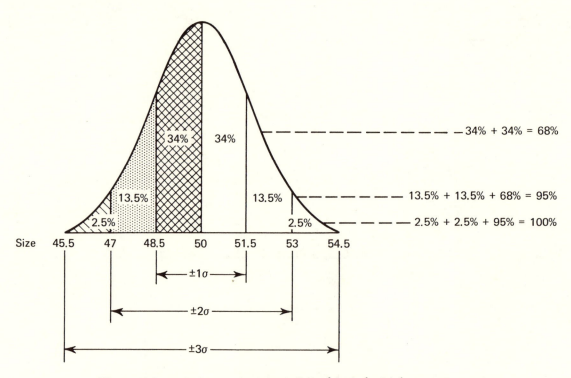

Figure II-3. Normal curve representation of an industrial process.

The terms of Variation Coefficient, V, and Standard Deviation, σ, are measures of variability of the distribution, which will be discussed later.

Measurement of Variability

Measurement of variability is a key to effective analysis of experiments and is particularly useful in assessing experimental error. The most widely applicable measure is the Standard Deviation, σ.

In order to illustrate the calculation of this value, let us assume that we have obtained the following tensile strengths, in pounds, by testing wire strips to be used for precision springs:

$$48$$

$$52$$

$$49$$

$$\underline{51}$$

Total, ΣX_i 200

No. of Tests, n = 4

Arithmetic Mean, $\overline{X}$

$= \Sigma X_i/n = 200/4$ 50

Here the symbol Σ is the capital Greek Sigma, meaning "Sum of" and each X_i represents one test result. The sum of the individual four X's is thus 200, and the arithmetic mean or "average" of the four outcomes is $\overline{X}$ = 200/4 or 50. These are familiar calculations to most. The symbols are given not because they are needed here, but because in many other literature references that you may wish to consult in the future, you will come across them and should be able to recognize and understand them on sight.

For convenience -- although not really necessary -- we might array our test results in ascending order of magnitude:

$$48$$
$$49$$
$$51$$
$$\underline{52}$$

Total: 200   Mean: 50

Next, we can ascertain in the deviations of each test value from the mean of 50, as shown on the following page: (Ignore column "C" for the moment.)

(a) Tensile Strength, Lb. = X_i	(b) Deviation d from Arithmetic Mean of 50 Lb.	(c) Squared Deviations, = d^2
48	-2	4
49	-1	1
51	+1	1
52	+2	4
Totals	$\Sigma d = 0$	$\Sigma d^2 = 10$

(handwritten: 48-50)

The deviations have added up to zero. In fact, so long as the calculations are not in error, the sum of the deviations from the mean will always be zero! If we square the deviations, however, as is done in column (c) we will get a non-zero total. In particular, (-2) times (-2) in the first row gives a +4; next $(-1)^2$ is +1, and the remaining two rows yield +1 and +4. The sum is +10. Dividing this 10 by the number of tests, 4, gives the average of the squared deviations, 10/4 = 2.5, also known as "variance" or $\sigma^2 = \dfrac{\Sigma d^2}{n}$. Another term that is sometimes applied is "mean square."

Observing that we used squares to obtain 2.5, it is only logical to now take the square root, yielding:

Standard Deviation, $\sigma = \sqrt{\text{variance}} = \sqrt{2.5} = 1.158$ or 1.6 rounded, in lb.

The standard deviation thus obtained is a measure of variability, the smaller its value, the less is the variation present. There are many advantages to this measure, the most important one being that a sample variance can be used to estimate the variance of the much larger lot as a whole. For this estimating purpose, however, one must use instead of n the term n-1 also known as Degrees of Freedom, DF. The basis of this procedure will be discussed shortly. For the example above then

Variance (as an estimate of population), $\sigma^2 = \Sigma d^2/(n-1) = 10/(4-1)$

$$= 3.33$$

and Standard Deviation, $\sigma = \sqrt{3.33} = 1.8$ lb.

The symbol is the widely used small Greek sigma, not to be confused with capital sigma Σ denoting "sum of."

In mathematical texts, a distinction is made between the standard deviation of a lot that is known from a very large number of tests (usually impractical to do from a cost time standpoint) and the estimate of σ from a quite small sample. This estimate may be shown by means of a prime, such as σ' or a caret ("hat"), $\hat{\sigma}$. While the student should be aware of these fine distinctions when reading various texts, it is also pointed out that the meaning of σ is usually clear from the context, and because of this the Workbook will dispense with either primes or carets, as really unnecessary except in more advanced work.

Variation Coefficient

It may have occurred to you that the Standard Deviation may be expressed as a percentage of the arithmetic mean. For the illustration just given, with:

Arithmetic Mean = 50 Pounds of Tensile Strength

Standard Deviation = 1.6 Pounds of Tensile Strength

we would find that the relative Standard Deviation, in percent, is simply (100 x 1.6)/50 = 3.2 percent. The value so obtained is the Coefficient of Variation or Variation Coefficient for short. More formally, we have:

Variation Coefficient, V, in percent

$$V = 100 \times \text{Standard Deviation/Arithmetic Mean}$$

$$V = 100 \times \frac{\sigma}{X}$$

For the example data

$$V = 100 \times \frac{1.6}{50} = 3.2 \text{ percent}$$

The advantage of the Variation Coefficient is that it expresses variability in the relative terms of a percentage, thus making it comparable regardless of the units of measurements (be they pounds of tensile strength, degrees of temperature, or micro-inches of thickness).

Note that the Variation Coefficient may be a percent of a percent. For example, for a shipment of insulating material, the percentage of allowable binder-admixture was given as 1 percent with a Standard Deviation of 0.2 percent. Converting these two figures to the single figure of variation coefficient, we have:

$$V, \% = 100 \times \frac{\sigma}{X}$$

$$= 100 \times \frac{0.2\%}{1\%}$$

$$= 20 \text{ percent}$$

Here the 20 percent is in terms of "percentage of percent binder-admixture." While the careless use of "percent of percent" is often dangerous and misleading, it is commonly accepted and valid for the variation coefficient as just illustrated.

ASSIGNMENT II-1:

Assume that we had tested a sample of 5 spring wires for tensile strength, each part having been selected at random. The results, in terms of observed pounds of strength appear next. Fill in the blank spaces, leading to Standard Deviation and Variation Coefficient as estimates of the population values.

Observed Test Result Strength in Lb.	Deviation from Mean, d	Squared Deviation, d^2
48	-2	4
49	-1	1
50	0	0
51	1	1
52	2	4
Totals	0	10

Mean, $\overline{X} = \Sigma x_i/n = 50$. $\sigma^2 = \Sigma d^2/(n-1) = 10/4 = 2.5$

Next, we find:

a. Standard Deviation

$$\sigma = \sqrt{\text{variance}} = \sqrt{\sigma^2} = \sqrt{2.5} = 1.58$$

b. Variation Coefficient

$$V, \% = \frac{100 \times \text{Standard Deviation}}{\text{Mean}} = \frac{100 \times \sigma}{\overline{X}} = 3.16\%$$

ASSIGNMENT II-2:

The research department of a tire manufacturer has developed a new tread design, which is thought to be safer, by requiring a smaller (shorter) stopping distance at 60 miles per hour than has been possible until now. Before deciding to go into mass production, a small lot of the new tires was produced on a pilot basis. Six sets of tires were checked for stopping distance, and the results for these six sets are given next.

Set No.	Stopping Distance, feet	Deviation from Mean	Squared Deviation
1	190	30	900
2	150	-10	100
3	170	10	100
4	160	0	0
5	130	-30	900
6	160	0	0
Total	960	xxxx	2000
Mean	160	xxxx	$\sigma^2 =$ 400

Obviously, many questions and problems must be solved before it is possible to make a good decision as to whether or not the new tire ought to be adopted for regular production. We are not ready, at this stage, to answer all these questions. We can, however, inform the management of the following data derived from the pilot run and the stopping distance test results:

a. The average stopping distance, in feet at 60 miles per hour (for the type of vehicle tested) is _____ 160 ft

b. The variation observed is as follows:

    (1) Variance, in feet^2 400

    (2) Standard Deviation, in feet   20

    (3) Coefficient of variation, in percent   12,5

Observe particularly that we may test a variety of types of vehicles, which may result in different average distances, but if the relation of Standard Deviation to average distance is constant, then the Coefficient of Variation will remain unchanged.

ASSIGNMENT II-3:

Assume the following test results for stopping distance in feet were found for the new tire tread design; all at 60 miles per hour:

	Average	Standard Deviation	Variation Coefficient
Ordinary passenger car	150	15	10
Station Wagon	120	12	10

	Average	Standard Deviation	Variation Coefficient
Truck, light	100	1.0	10
Truck, medium	80	0.8	10
Truck, heavy	70	0.7	10

Insert the variation coefficient in the blank space provided above.

ASSIGNMENT II-4:

Referring to the data just given for the 5 different types of vehicles, assume that in each case the Standard Deviation had been 1.0 feet. Find the variation coefficients:

Ordinary passenger car: .67 %.   Station Wagon .83 %.

Light Truck: 10 %.   Medium Truck: 1.25 %.   Heavy Truck: 1.428 %.

Degrees of Freedom in Sampling

We have defined Standard Deviation, as applicable in obtaining an indicator of variability. However, as an estimator of the variability in the lot as a whole, the sample Standard Deviation involves a slight downward bias, because the lot Standard Deviation is usually a little larger than the sample Standard Deviation as compared above. In order to correct for this bias, it is merely necessary in the computations to divide the sum of the squared deviations by the quantity n-1, instead of n. The mathematical justification of this procedure is quite complex, and the reader who wishes to check on the theoretical proof should refer to advanced texts in the field. For reasons that are not fully clear, the accepted term for n - 1 is "Degrees of Freedom."

The effect of using Degrees of Freedom, DF, is to increase the estimate of the population variance. In our original example for n = 4 tensile strengths with a sum of squared deviations of 10, we thus have:

Biased estimate of variance = 10/4 = 2.5

Unbiased estimate of variance, σ^2 = 10/3 = 3.33

with respective standard deviations of 1.6 and 1.8 in pounds.

A justification for the use of DF in place of n may also be given in intuitive terms, along the following reasoning:

a. In those rare instances when the statistician has data representing the population as a whole, he knows the population mean simply by adding all the values and dividing the total so found by the number N of values in the lot.

b. The statistician then simply calculates:

Population variance $\sigma^2 = \Sigma(X_i - \text{Mean})^2/N$

c. When dealing with a sample, however, we do not know the population mean. Instead we estimate it from the sample values. Then:

Estimated population variance $\sigma^2 = \Sigma(X_i - \overline{X})/DF$

where DF = n-1 allows for the fact that we have used an estimate of the population mean.

It should also be noted that a population is considered theoretically infinite, but in practice the sampling estimate will work well so long as N is equal to or greater than 10n; that is, the lot size is at least ten times the sample size. For other situations, which are almost never encountered in practical experimentation, additional adjustments apply.

It should also be realized that when n is greater than 25, the difference in effect between this value and DF begins to diminish rapidly.

Finite Lot Size

An experimenter, who has produced, say, 10 pilot units of a new invention, might conclude: "I have invented a new item, and tested it for its various quality and lift characteristics. My sample size is 10, and so is my lot size, since these 10 units are all that exists in the whole word." Next, in obtaining the Standard Deviation, he will use N and not N-1, because he feels he is dealing with the lot or "universe" or total "population" of units. ─produce more then infinite size at later date.

After some reflection, such reasoning will surely be found faulty. Admittedly, there are only 10 units around at the present. But the purpose of these units and the purpose of the tests performed on them is not just to evaluate this entire group, but to predict the quality and life characteristics of future units to be made in a manner patterned according to the information revealed by the 10 pilot units. The units that can be made in the future and indeed may be made are for all practical purposes indefinitely large and comparable to an "infinite" population at least conceptually.* The pilot units must be viewed as a sample of this universe.

─────────────────────

*Note that the words "indefinitely large" and "infinite" refer to a practically indistinct limit.

FUNDAMENTALS OF STATISTICAL ANALYSIS OF EXPERIMENTS

ASSIGNMENT II-5:

The purpose of this assignment is to show how small the differences in effect become when n is larger than 25. In this example, for noise level readings in db above 50 for an electric motor, n = 31 and hence DF = 30.

X_i	Frequency f of Observation	fX_i	d	d^2	fd^2	
2	2	4	-2	4	8	The mean $\overline{X}$ = 124/31
3	8	24	-1	1	8	
4	12	48	0	0	0	= 4
5	6	30	1	1	6	
6	3	18	2	4	12	
Totals	31	124	0	-	34	

The unbiased variance and standard deviation are 34/30 = 1.13 and 1.065, respectively; while the biased values are 34/31 = 1.097 and 1.047 respectively.

Thus the bias (underestimate) is ___2%___ percent.

Comparing Precision of Instruments

The variation coefficient is often of value when comparing the relative precision of test instruments. For example, nondestructive testing of the density of concrete surfaces is done with a nuclear gauge, measuring the amount of backscatter produced.

Three nuclear gauges, A, B and C were tested for relative precision by making repeat tests on the same concrete block. The less variability in successive tests, the more precise is that instrument.

A typical set of tests results in terms of backscatter counts appears in Table II-1. We observe that the instrument averages differ. Such differences are common but of no concern to the tester, since the calibration procedure (correlating the instrument counts to known physical density values) automatically adjusts for the average level of each instrument. Thus the investigators' interests center around the observed variability from repeat measurements, which serves as an indicator of relative precision. Now, since the instrument averages differ considerably, but will be of no practical importance, it is apparent that not the standard deviation but rather the Variation Coefficient* should be compared. The latter, resulting from the ratio of Standard Deviation to Arithmetic Average, should be comparable in relative terms.

*The calculation steps given for finding the Standard Deviation are somewhat different from those previously shown, and are known as the so-called shortcut procedure, which is a shortcut only when a relatively large numbe of data must be checked. Students who have a desk calculator available can readily check and verify that the results -- barring arithmetical error -- are identical by the ordinary and shortcut methods.

We note (Table II-1) that Instruments A and B have approximately similar Coefficients of 1.3 and 1.2 percent. This Variation Coefficient is a measure of precision or "instrument error." Device C has a notably lower Coefficient of 0.8 percent, and must thus be considered the most precise by exhibiting the smallest instrument error. If it had not been for the difference in averages, we would have been able to utilize the Standard Deviations to compare precision.

ASSIGNMENT II-6:

Compute the Standard Deviations for the three nuclear gages by the ordinary (long) method and compare the results (which should be identical) with the shortcut method.

Standard Deviations by:	Gage A	Gage B	Gage C
Shortcut Method	1.3	1.2	0.8
Ordinary (long) method	___	___	___

Observe in passing that a further question -- which we are not as yet ready to answer -- is whether the difference between gages A and B, and A and C, and B and C is significant and not just ascribable to chance fluctuation of sampling. We will come back to this question in a later chapter.

ASSIGNMENT II-7:

Assuming that a desk calculator is not available, use the shortcut approach to calculate the unbiased Standard Deviation for the data below.

Tensile, lb $= X$	(Tensile, lb)^2 $= X^2$
8	64
9	81
11	121
12	144
$\Sigma X =$ _40_	$\Sigma X^2 =$ _410_

Table II-1

COMPARATIVE PRECISIONS OF THREE NUCLEAR DENSITY TESTING DEVICES

Backscatter Counts

Instrument Reading	Instrument A	Instrument B	Instrument C
1	498	612	1216
2	501	607	1203
3	511	618	1220
4	506	599	1198
5	499	604	1203
a. Total, ΣX	2515	3040	6040
b. Mean $= \Sigma X/n = \Sigma X/5$	503	608	1208
c. DF $= n-1 = 5-1$	4	4	4
d. ΣX^2	1,265,163	1,848,534	7,296,678
e. $(\Sigma X)^2/n = (\Sigma X)^2/5$	1,265,045	1,848,320	7,296,320
f. SS * $= d - e =$ $\Sigma X^2 - (\Sigma X)^2/N$	118	214	358
g. Variance $= \sigma^2 = f/c =$ SS/DF $=$ SS/4	29.5	53.5	89.5
h. Std. Deviation $= \sigma = \sqrt{g}$	5.4	7.3	9.5
i. Variation Coefficient, $V =$ $100\sigma/$ Mean, in percent	1.1	1.2	0.8

---

*SS = of Squares in the formula: Variance = (Sum of Squares) / DF

Note: The variance has been calculated by the so-called shortcut method, which avoids the need to square individual deviations. For example, for Instrument A, the deviations of the individual values from the Mean 503 are: 498 - 503 = -5, 501 - 503 = -2, 511 - 503 = 8, 506 - 503 = 3, and 499 - 503 = -4. Next, squaring and summing these differences, we obtain 25 + 4 + 64 + 9 + 16 = 118. This total corresponds to the Sum of Squares found above. All subsequent calculations remain unchanged.

$$\sigma^2 = \frac{\text{Sum of Squares of Sample Measurents} - \left(\frac{\text{Sum of Measurem...}}{n}\right)}{n-1}$$

$$\text{SD or } \sigma = \sqrt{\sigma^2} \qquad = \Sigma x^2 - (\Sigma x)^2/n$$

Next:

a.   DF = n-1 = ___4___ - ___1___ = ___3___ .

b. ΣX^2 = __410__   and c. $(\Sigma X)^2/n$ = _1600_ /4 = _400_ .

d.   Sum of Squares = b - c = _410_ - _400_ = _10_ .

e.   Variance = (Sum of Squares)/DF = d/a = _10_ / _3_ = _3.33_ .

f.   Standard Deviation = $\sqrt{\text{Variance}}$ = _1.82_ .

    Your answer, to be correct, should be 1.8. This result is identical to the Standard Deviation found in the section on <u>Degrees of Freedom in Sampling</u> earlier in this chapter, for the spring wire tensile strengths of 48, 49, 51 and 52 pounds. For simplicity in squaring, the data just given were reduced in size by subtracting the magnitude 40 pounds from each, thus giving the 8, 9, 11 and 12 above. Such subtraction of a constant is known as coding. Coded data give Standard Deviations identical to those of the original uncoded ones, as you will note, by simply comparing both σ's.

    In order to complete the definitions, we may note that the quantity ΣX^2 may be called "Gross Sum of Squares," with the term $(\Sigma X)^2/N$ known as the "Correction Factor." Subtracting the Correction Factor from the Gross Sum of Squares yields the "Sum of Squares," which is divided by the Degrees of Freedom to arrive at the "Meansquare," which is also the variance. Thus far the terms Meansquare and Variance have been used interchangeably, but in subsequent statistical analyses the two terms may designate slightly different types of variations, as will be shown.

Calculating Experimental Error Term

    We now have acquired sufficient background to calculate the Standard Deviation representing the error term in an experiment. Figure II-4 shows the yield, in percent, obtained in an investigation of the effect of type of machine setting (A and B) and operating speed (low and high). A replication of two was involved, so that each condition or cell, representing a factor-level combination, contains two yields.

    For simplification, we will code the data by subtracting 90 from each yield entry. Next we will find the Variance in each of the 4 cells. It is apparent that the average Variance represents the error term, since it is derived from the differences in yield observed between the two replicated experimental runs. Unknown "chance-type" variations must have caused these differences, which are therefore considered to represent random error or experimental error. The square root of the

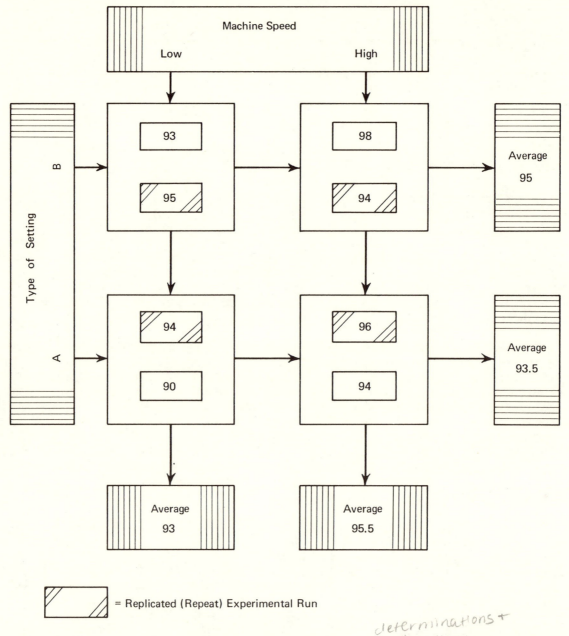

= Replicated (Repeat) Experimental Run

Figure II-4: Yield, in percent, from two machine settings and speeds. *determinations + replications*

4 conditions
2 observ. for each condition

average Variance is the Standard Deviation representing Experimental Error. The detailed procedure, utilizing the regular method for unbiased estimation of Variance, is shown by the successive steps given in the schematic form of Figure II-5.

Some care will be required to follow all the steps, but there should be no real problem of understanding the procedures. We are merely applying our known techniques to a specific new type of problem.

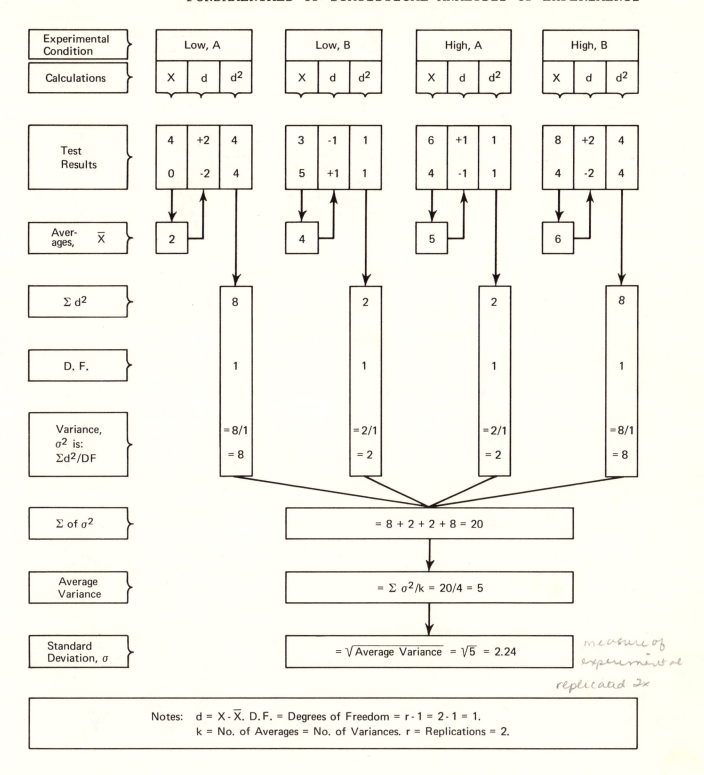

Figure II-5: Estimation of experimental-error Standard Deviation by calculating the average of the Variances for the replicated test results.

The Standard Deviation found is 2.24, in terms of yield. Whether or not this magnitude may be considered relatively large (or small) for this experiment will become clear only after testing its significance (to be shown in the next chapter).

ASSIGNMENT II-8:

The tin plate problem of Assignment I-10 involved 3 labs, A, B, M, 3 tin sheet strips, and 3 discs per lab and strip combination. Because of time limitations, however, only 2 discs were tested per condition (lab-strip combination) so that the number of replications was 2. The data, in hundredths of a gram, appear below, together with the initial calculations of the error Standard Deviation. Complete the job.

	Strip 1			Strip 2			Strip 3			
	A	B	M	A	B	M	A	B	M	Total
1st Test, X_1	81	81	81	82	81	84	87	83	81	
2nd Test, X_2	83	81	81	86	81	82	85	81	81	
Mean, X	82	81	81	84	81	83	86	82	81	
Deviation, d, from X_1	-1	0	0	-2	0	1	1	1	0	
Deviation, d, from X_2	1	0	0	2	0	-1	-1	-1	0	
d_1 squared	1	0	0	4	0	1	1	1	0	
d_2 squared	1	0	0	4	0	1	1	1	0	
Sum of d^2 = SS (add prior two squares)	2	0	0	8	0	2	2	2	0	
Degrees Freedom, N - 1	1	1	1	1	1	1	1	1	1	
(Sum of d^2)/(N-1) = Variance	2	0	0	8	0	2	2	2	0	16

If you do not obtain a total of 16 for the last column, representing the addition of the 9 individual variances for each laboratory and strip combination, then recheck. The remaining steps are simple:

1. The average of the 9 variances is 16/9 = _____ 1.78

2. The Standard Deviation is $\sqrt{16/9}$ = _____ 1.33

This is the experimental error expressed in the form of Standard Deviation. The data were in hundredths of a gram, to avoid the problem of squaring decimals above. We now convert to grams by dividing the Standard Deviation by 100. Therefore:

3. Standard Deviation, in grams, is ___1.33/100 = .0133___

ASSIGNMENT II-9: Review Problem

In order to assess the effect of high and low forming pressure, for two machines, I and II, on the hardness in 100's of Degrees Knopp of glass bead, the following 3-replicate experiment was run:

	Machine I	Machine II
Low Pressure	2　2　2	3　5　4
High Pressure	4　8　6	6　4　5

The tabulation below may be of help in finding the experimental error. Complete the entries.

	Low Pressure		High Pressure		Total
	I	II	I	II	
1st Test	2	3	4	6	
2nd Test	2	5	8	4	
3rd Test	2	4	6	5	
Arithmetic Mean	2	4	6	5	
Deviations, d	0	-1	-2	1	
	0	1	2	-1	
	0	0	0	0	
Squared Deviations, d^2	0	1	4	1	
	0	1	4	1	
	0	0	0	0	
Sum of Squared Deviations	0	2	8	2	
Degrees Freedom, N-1	2	2	2	2	3 tests
$\sigma^2 = d^2/(N-1)$	0	1	4	1	

Having obtained these values, we now follow these further final steps:

1. Average of the Variances is ___6___ / ___4___ or ___1.5___ .

2. Standard Deviation of experimental error: ___1.22___ in 100's of Knopp.

Summary

Statistics is the science concerned with evaluating the behavior of measurements, such as we obtain from reading test results or acquiring other types of observations regarding materials, products, operations or performances. Principally, this evaluation is centered around the assessment of averages and variation around these averages, as well as the conclusions to be drawn from the results.

We have learned how to calculate the Standard Deviation and the related value of Variation Coefficient as the principal and most widely used indexes of variability. Next, we have made some initial applications of our knowledge to evaluate precision of testing instruments and to state the amount of experimental error in research studies.

Thus far we have made only a beginning. As was already indicated, we need to also judge the relative significance of test averages and variations, or else we are unable to readily evaluate whether or not a certain experimental error is large and whether or not certain differences in experimental effects might be merely reflections of chance fluctuations and thus not of real importance.

You are asked to stick with us for this further study. You may desire, first, to review the material covered thus far. Do not worry if not everything is crystal clear. Such is the usual occurrence in any in-depth learning process. As you continue with the further material, earlier parts that may seem fuzzy will tend to fall in line. An occasional review, also, will be helpful.

Chapter III

ASCERTAINING THE SIGNIFICANCE OF OUTCOMES

Once an investigation has been conducted in accordance with the best feasible design, and the experimental error has been evaluated, the next step is to assess the significance of the outcomes observed, as will be discussed now.

Significance of Differences

An experiment yields averages that can be shown in tabular and graphic form. For our previous investigation of the effect of machines and settings on production yield, we obtain these averages:

Machine Speeds

	Low			High			Setting Average
	Run 1	Run 2	Average	Run 1	Run 2	Average	
Setting B:	95	93	94	98	94	96	95
Setting A:	90	94	92	94	96	95	93.5
Machine Average			93			95.5	

$1+1+1+4+4+4+1+1$ $\frac{20}{4} = 5\sigma^2$ $\sigma = \sqrt{5}$

Since graphs reveal a great deal of readily comprehensible information, it is desirable to graph the experimental outcomes, as shown in Figure III-1.

The question is: Are the differences in the averages significant or not? Non-significance indicates that the experimental evidence accumulated is not enough to arrive at a firm conclusion. The observed differences in averages may be merely the result of chance fluctuations -- like the luck-of-the-draw in sampling, inherent imperfections in test procedures or instrumentation, or other causes in the nature of experimental error. Recall that experimental error variations are of a nature and magnitude considered unavoidable under good care, thus distinct from mistakes.

Unless the differences in averages exceed the effects ascribable to likely experimental error, our results cannot be considered as having provided significant findings. Experimental chance variations could also have produced some differences in averages. The problem is not academic. Many misleading conclusions have been reported from industrial, scientific, medical and social research investigations merely because the experimenters mistook chance occurrences for "real."

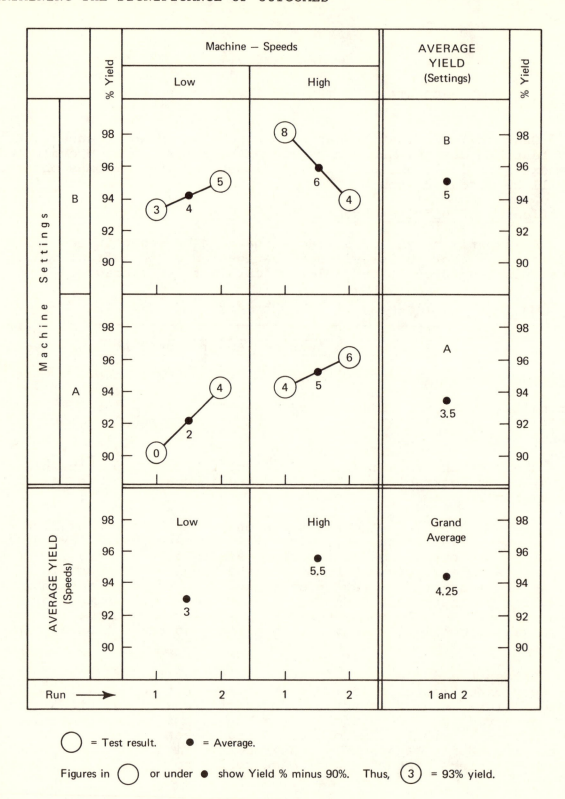

= Test result.   ● = Average.

Figures in ◯ or under ● show Yield % minus 90%. Thus, ③ = 93% yield.

Figure III-1: Graph of tests results. Individuals and averages are plotted. Thus, for setting B at low speed, the two experimental runs (replications) yielded 93 and 95 percent, with an overage of 94. A general trend for increased yield from low to high speed and from setting B to setting A is noted.

Steps in Evaluating Significance of Difference

A number of relatively simple steps accomplish an evaluation of the differences among observed averages. For the speed-settings data, it is apparent that we would wish to compare (1) differences between the two speeds, (2) differences between the two settings, and (3) differences among the four conditions representing speed-setting combinations.

A tabular procedure will illustrate the evaluation, below.

Step No.	Procedure	Average Under Comparison			Experiment Error Term
		Speeds	Settings	Speed-Setting Combinations	
1.	No. k of average under comparison	2	2	4	
2.	Highest average	95.5	95.0	96.0	
3.	Lowest average	93.0	93.5	92.0	
4.	Difference in averages, (2) - (3)	2.5	1.5	4.0	
5.	Experimental error standard deviation (as found previously in Chapter II), σ				2.24
6.	Sample size n, representing the number of observations from which each average was obtained	4	4	2	
7.	$\sqrt{n}$ =	2	2	1.41	
8.	Standard deviation of averages, $\sigma_{\bar{x}}$ (known as "sigma-sub-x-bar" or "standard error of the mean") = $\sigma/\sqrt{n}$ = (5)/(7)	1.12	1.12	1.6	
9.	Degrees of Freedom DF associated with the experimental error standard deviation [With a replication of 2, per each of the four cells, error Degrees of Freedom are 4 x (2 - 1) = 4]				4.0
10.	Factor q from Table 3, Appendix	3.9	3.9	5.8	
11.	Confidence Interval, CI, based on CI = q x $\sigma_{\bar{x}}$ = (10)(8)	4.4	4.4	9.3	
12.	Is difference of Step 4 equal to or greater than CI?	No	No	No	
13.	Are differences between means significant at 95 Percent Confidence Level?	No	No	No	

[handwritten notes: "Chance variation can be as high as ... with 95% confidence" next to step 11 Speeds column; "only 5 will exceed 4.4" at right of step 11]

The conclusions are obvious: Although there is a greater observed yield for Setting A and for high machine speeds, these improvements are found not to be significant at the 95 percent confidence level. Chance fluctuations of sampling and testing, and other experimental errors could well have produced these effects. On the other hand, if, in Step 12, the observed differences in any of the three sets of comparisons had equaled or exceeded the Confidence Interval CI, we would have judged this significant at the 95 percent level. Other CI's are obtained with different confidence levels (and corresponding tabular values q), but 95 is the most frequently used level, in percent.

In the event that the differences between the speed-setting combination means had been shown statistically significant, then other differences among the individual means also require evaluation. For example, is the average of 95 for high speed, setting B significantly higher than 92 for low speed, setting A? In the present case we know that it is not, because the difference of 96 - 92 = 4 is not significant, and thus the smaller difference is surely not significant (95 - 92 = 3).

Further Points

Note that a distinction must be made between the experimental error standard deviation, σ or σ_{error}, and the standard error of the mean $\sigma_{\overline{x}}$, as shown by Lines 5 and 8 above.

One might claim that significance testing is not really necessary in practical situations, because engineers' and others personal judgments based on extensive experience are a good substitute. There is, however, a distinction between technical aspects of differences and statistical ones. Only the latter can take proper account of the effect of sample size and inherent experimental error variation to come up with a quantitative evaluation. Particularly in borderline situations or where managers, technical personnel and supervisors disagree, is a objective assessment of value. Moreover, one critical aspect of our age of ever-accelerating technological advances is that people have less and less time in which to develop that degree of "expertise" that permit a claim of "adequate familiarity" with a product or process to make "experienced judgments." When traveling in uncharted territory we need good soundings of the water level. Significance testing with Confidence Intervals then becomes an essential aid in the managerial and engineering decision process. Judgments made without such tests can lead to costly errors, such as making costly changes in product designs, materials specifications, or processing equipments and arrangements -- based on chance rather than real information extracted from the experiment.

Concepts in Significance Testing

Certain ~~of the~~ concepts of significance testing required further discussion:

1. <u>Standard Error of the Mean</u> - You may have correctly guessed that Standard Error again refers to variability or error in measurements. This time, however, it relates to <u>variation in sample averages</u>. The Standard Deviation is a measure of variation in individual tests, while the Standard Error refers to variation that may be expected in sample averages. A function of the sample size, n, this measure states:

compare avgs.

$$\text{Std. Error, } \sigma_{\bar{x}} = \sigma / \sqrt{n,}$$

The term is particularly important in quality control work.

2. <u>Experimental Unit</u> - The individual test results -- breaking strengths in pounds, dimensions in inches, efficiencies in percent, temperatures in degrees or yield in percent, etc. -- that constitute the outcomes of an experiment are known also as the "experimental units" or "sampling units." We had 8 such units in the speeds-settings experiment. There were 2 units per cell, and 4 cells representing the 4 machine and speed combinations or conditions, giving a total of 2 x 4 = 8.

Confidence Interval

When the Standard Error is multiplied by the appropriate factor, q, we obtain a quality known as Confidence Interval, CI. These factors, based on confidence level of 95 percent, are given in the Appendix and are due to E.S. Pearson and H.O. Hartley. For example, when we found a CI of 4.4 for the Speed Averages, this is what it meant:

> "Based on the inherent experimental error varia-
> tion in this investigation, we may expect a differ-
> ence between the two speed averages of the experi-
> ment at a magnitude of up to 4.4 some 95 percent
> of the time. Therefore, if the observed difference
> is less than this 4.4, it must be ascribed to chance
> Fluctuations."

In other words, only if an observed difference is greater than CI will we have established its significance.

The choice of a 95 percent Confidence Level is based on predominant custom. Practice has shown it to be most suitable for industrial experimentation. Tables of q-factors for 90 percent and 99 percent Confidence Levels are available in many texts*. It will be apparent that <u>q for the 90 percent level is smaller than q for 95 percent</u>. Conversely, for the 99 percent level it is larger.

---

*Originally published in <u>Biometrika Tables</u>, Cambridge University Press, 1956.

Observe also that q decreases with increasing DF. This is logical. A greater DF means more evidence (sampling units) have been gathered, thus a relatively smaller CI will now suffice to establish significance.

Significance

When we have demonstrated significance at a certain level, such as 95 percent confidence, we have an assurance with odds of 20 to 1 that the outcomes under comparison are real. There remains, of course, a 5 percent or 1 in 20 chance or risk of erroneously calling a difference "real." In other words, 5 times out of 100 when a significance test comes out positive, this will occur in error as a result of the chance fluctuations of sampling, testing, instrument variability, surrounding test conditions, human variability and related random factors.

Now, when an experiment comes out "not significant," there is of course also a certain possibility that chance fluctuations have fooled us and that there really is a difference among the averages. One alternative left to us, when the verdict from an experiment comes out non-significant, is to do some more replications. This further investigative work yields additional data, thus accumulating further evidence. If there is a real difference among the averages, then this additional data may well serve to point it up. Before undertaking additional replications, however, there must be a weighing of the potential value of the results anticipated against the time and cost expenditures.

ASSIGNMENT III-1:

For convenience of reference, there are reproduced below the 2-replicate tin plate experiment data, for Laboratories A, B and M and Strips 1, 2 and 3.

	Laboratory A			Laboratory B			Laboratory M			Strip Average
	Test 1	Test 2	Avg.	Test 1	Test 2	Avg.	Test 1	Test 2	Avg.	
Strip 1:	81	83	82	81	81	81	81	81	81	81.25
Strip 2:	82	86	84	81	81	81	84	82	83	82.67
Strip 3:	87	85	86	83	81	82	81	81	81	83.00
Lab. Average			84			81.33			81.67	

1. Now complete the tabulation below, leading to an evaluation of significance:

	Laboratories	Strips	Strip-Lab. Combinations
1. No., k, of average being compared	3	3	9
2. Difference between Highest and Lowest Average	2.67	1.67	.5

	Laboratories	Strips	Strip-Lab. Combinations	Experimental Error Term
3. Standard Deviation				1.33
4. No., n, of original test results (= experimental units) from which each average was obtained)	6	6	2	
5. Standard Error	.54	.54	.94	
6. Degrees of Freedom (=DF per cell x N. of cells)			$9 \times (2-1)$	9
7. Factor q from Table (Appendix)	4	4	5.6	
8. CI = q x Std. Error	2.16	2.16	5.26	
9. Significant at 95% Confidence? Yes/No	95% Yes	No	No	

$1.33/\sqrt{n}$ (row 5 margin note)

are sgn. (note below row 9 Laboratories)

may be signif at 90% (margin note by Strip-Lab. Combinations)

2. Now, utilizing the CI found for laboratory averages, compare all 3 laboratories against each other, entering the difference among averages below. Circle those that are significant (that is, greater than the CI for laboratories found):

		Lab. A	Lab. B	Lab. M
	Average	84	81.3	81.7
Lab. A	84	0	(2.7)	(2.3)
Lab. B	81.3	omit	0	.4
Lab. M	81.7	omit	omit	0

A & B
A & M

The omitted items, you will note, would represent repetition.

3. Repeat the analysis, this time for Strips.

		Strip 1	Strip 2	Strip 3
	Average	81.3	82.7	83.0
Strip 1:	81.3	0	1.4	1.7
Strip 2:	82.7	omit	0	.3
Strip 3:	83.0	omit	omit	0

As a result of this work, you will have identified, at the 95 percent confidence level, those factors and averages that are significantly different. In this manner, you will have indicated areas where something may be in need of improvement, often through further checks and investigations. Differences between laboratories, if significant, may be ascribable to test procedures, methods, instruments and similar factors among laboratories. Differences between strips may point to non-uniformity of operation of the tin plating process or variations in the tin sheet itself, that need to be rectified.

4. Now enlarge the comparisons to include the individual laboratory-strip average combinations:

		Strip 1			Strip 2			Strip 3		
		A	B	M	A	B	M	A	B	M
	Average	82	81	81	84	81	83	86	82	81
Strip 1 A	82	0	1	1	2	1	1	4	0	1
1 B	81		0	0	3	0	2	5	1	0
1 M	81			0	3	0	2	5	1	0
Strip 2 A	84				0	3	1	2	2	3
2 B	81					0	2	5	1	0
2 M	83						0	3	1	2
Strip 3 A	86							0	4	5
3 B	82								0	1
3 M	81									0

more significant

◯ = significant

Circle those differences that equal or exceed the Confidence Interval.

CI = 2.16 Labs   CI = 2.16 Strips   CI = 5.26 Strip-Labs

ASSIGNMENT III-2:

Previously, we investigated the effect of high and low forming pressure and two machines (I and II) on glass bead hardness. This 3-replicate study gave these results:

	Machine I	Machine II
Low Pressure:	2,2,2; Avg. 2	3,5,4; Avg. 4
High Pressure:	4,8,6; Avg. 6	6,4,5; Avg. 5

Machine I Low: 0   Machine II Low: 3
Machine I High: 4   Machine II High: 5.5, 4.5
High avg: 4

1. Are the effects of pressure significant? Also, does it make a difference whether machine I or II is used? We proceed

$0 + 4 + ? = \frac{6}{4} = 1.5$

as follows (complete the form provided):

	Pressures	Machines	Machine-Pressure Combinations
1. No., k of averages compared	2	2	4
2. Difference between highest and lowest average	2.5	.5	4
3. Standard Deviation	1.22	1.22	1.22
4. No. of experimental units per Average, n	6	6	3
5. Standard Error $\sigma/\sqrt{n}$	.498	.498	.704
6. Degrees of Freedom	8	8	8
7. Factor q from Table	3.3	3.3	4.4
8. CI = q x Std. Error	1.6434	1.6434	3.0976
9. Significant at 95% Yes/No	Yes	No	Yes

(no† of cells) x
(DF for cond)
4 x (3-1)

2. Now compare the Machine-Pressure combinations separately (provided the answer in Question 1, Part 9, was "yes" for these averages).

		Machine I		Machine II	
		Low	High	Low	High
	Average	2	6	4	5
Machine I Low	2	0	(4)	2	3
Machine I High	6		0	2	1
Machine II Low	4			0	1
Machine II High	5				0

3. These glass beads are used for industrial processing applications, that call for a high degree of hardness (aside, of course, from other characteristics , such as a minimum of out-of-roundness, close control of diameter, etc.). Based on the experiment results, what are your recommendations?

(a) The most desirable pressure is _not certain_ (insert high, low or not certain), because _____ at 95% CI .

(b) As regards the difference in hardness obtained by the two machines, it is found that _higher hardness on machine I_ Non significant difference in machines

(Your recommendation here will depend on whether the higher hardness on Machine II is significant.)

Short-Cut Method in Significance Testing

When evaluating significance of difference among experimental averages, the most time consuming calculation is usually the estimation. There exists a short-cut method utilizing Ranges. Somewhat approximate, the procedure is nevertheless quite suitable for many purposes in industrial and other research work. If the Range method leads to a borderline case of either significance or non-significance, one can still resort to the long, precise method of estimating the Standard Deviation from the squared deviations.

The Range is the difference between the highest and lowest test result (or experimental unit) in a cell. For the speeds-settings experiment, where there were only 2 units per cell, the Range is simply the difference between them. For the four cells, we have:

Factor-Level Combination	Yields from Runs 1 and 2	Range, R = Difference
B and Low	93 and 95	2
A and Low	94 and 90	4
B and High	98 and 94	4
A and High	96 and 94	2
Total, ΣR		12
Average Range, $\overline{R} = \Sigma R/k = 12/4$		3

The symbol k denotes the number of ranges comprising the total of all R's. An approximate estimate of the Standard Deviation, which is about 80 percent as reliable as the estimate* from the squared-deviations method, is now obtained from the following procedure:

1. State the Average Range, $\overline{R}$ 3

2. Give the sample size, n, from which each Range, R, was obtained   2

   (Note: Be sure not to confuse sample size, n, with number of samples, k.)

3. From the Conversion Factors, F_d Table in the Appendix, find F_d for n = 2:   0.9

---

*Both methods give estimates, since the true universe Standard Deviation is exactly known only in that instance when all the units of the universe (or lot or production) are tested. See also the discussion "Finite Lot Sizes" of Chapter II.

(Note: From quality control work, some students will recognize F_d as the reciprocal of the more widely published d_2^d devisors. We use the reciprocals, F_d, since in practice a multiplication is usually simpler than division.)

4. Multiply F_d x $\overline{R}$, thus obtaining the estimated (approximate) Standard Deviation of the experimental error. We find, 0.9 x 3 =   2.7

The Standard Deviation obtained by the longer, precise method is 2.24. The difference between the two is not large enough to affect our conclusions regarding significance.

ASSIGNMENT III-3:

Calculate the short-cut experimental error Standard Deviation for the glass bead experiment. The data are given in Assignment III-2.

1. Enter the data and find Ranges.

Factor-Level Combination	Hardness from 3 Runs			Range
	Run 1	Run 2	Run 3	
Low – MacI	2	2	2	0
Low – MacII	3	5	4	2
High – MacI	4	8	6	4
High – MacII	6	4	5	2
Total				8
Average Range, $\overline{R}$				2

2. Note the sample size per Range, n   3

3. Enter the appropriate Factor F_d .591

4. Find the estimated Standard Deviation from $\overline{R}$ x F_d 1.182

The approximate estimate of the Standard Deviation is now used in lieu of that previously found from the sums of squared deviations method in assessing significance of differences. One final observation: Just because the approximate Standard Deviation comes out different from the longer method does not mean that either is actually more accurate. We can never know at any given instance which Standard Deviation most closely reflects the unknown universe σ. But it can be proved by mathematical-statistical methods that, in the long run, the approximate method is about 80 percent as precise as the sums of squared-deviations σ in estimating the universe σ.*

---

*In statistical terminology, we usually refer to an estimate obtained through sampling as a statistic (not "statistics"), while the value of the universe that is being estimated is the parameter. In short, a statistic is a sampling estimate of the parameter.

ASCERTAINING THE SIGNIFICANCE OF OUTCOMES

Significance of Differences in Variation

Thus far, we have been concerned with comparisons among averages of experimental trial results. Sometimes, however, we have need to investigate whether or not the differences in variations are significant. For such purposes, we utilize the ratio of the variances involved and evaluate significance by means of a Table of Factors of Variance Ratio, F, in the Appendix. Unless the actual ratio of variances equals or exceeds the tabulated F, the difference must be considered as not significant.

The variation coefficients of 1.1, 1.2 and 0.8 for the three density gauges of Table II-1, when squared are known as relative variances. Thus for A, B and C, respectively, the relative variances are 1.21, 1.44 and 0.64, respectively. Let us see whether A and B differ significantly in precision:

1. For variances or relative variances, form a ratio of the greater to the smaller variance. Thus,

   F-ratio = (Greater Variance) / (Smaller Variance) = 1.44/1.21 = 1.19.

2. The Degrees of Freedom, DF, associated with the numerator is N-1 = 5-1 = 4. Similarly, for the denominator, DF = N-1 = 4. Use of this set of DF's to enter the F-ratio Table in the Appendix.

3. The critical ratio provided by the F Table is 6.4. For an observed ratio to be significant at the 95 percent confidence level, it must equal or exceed the critical ratio. In our case, the ratio 1.19 observed is well below the critical ratio of 6.4. Therefore, the difference in precision between instruments A and B is not significant.

ASSIGNMENT III-4:

Compare the relative variance of Gauge A with Gauge C, to evaluate significance.

1. Relative variance of A is: _____ 1.21

2. Relative variance of C is: _____ .64

3. Variance Ratio F; found by dividing relative variance of A by relative variance of C: _____ 1.89

4. Tabular F-ratio (this is the critical ratio) _____ 6.4

Can just use variance

$F_{OBS} > F_{table}$ then... significant

5. Significant? Yes/No   _No_

State your conclusion relative to the precision of the two gauges:

_____

_____

_____

_____

ASSIGNMENT III-5:

For the measurement of degree of compaction, in percent, two methods are available known as the "sand cone" and the "rubber balloon" test. Variances for the two are 2.8 and 2.2 percent respectively, based on 120 sand cone tests but only 30 rubber balloon tests. Although 120 rubber balloon tests had been scheduled , it was subsequently found that the last 90 had been conducted in a non-standard manner. Evaluate the precision, below:

1. F -ratio of the two actual variances   _1.27_

2. Tabulated F needed for significance   _≈ 1.70_

3. Significant? Yes/No   _No_

Again note that we test significance at the 95 percent level. For other levels (such as 90 or 99) consult tables available in most texts. It is of course almost axiomatic that a ratio that barely fails to be significant at the 95 percent level will be significant at least at the 90 percent level.

4. Discuss: Is the sand-cone method more precise?_____

_____ No because no significance — could be_____

_upperimental error_____

_____ _9.3_

_____ _2.965_____

_____

Not knowing how the two test methods are made may be an advantage, because one can then perform the statistical analysis in a more unbiased manner. Of course, a final evaluation also requires the judgment of the technologist who is familiar with the technical aspects of each method. The statistical method serves impartially anyone who knows how to apply it properly. Technological experience profiting by the judgment gained from practice, teamed with statistically valid evaluation constitute the ingredients of sound decisions.

ASSIGNMENT III-6: Review Problem

Hot forging of ingots in the production of billets requires careful attention to heating cycles and forging temperatures. Among the criteria of quality attained is the grain size of the billets. The following are results of a 3-replicate experiment in terms of grain size index from 3 heating cycles (A, B and C) and two temperatures (high and low).

Temperature		Heating Cycle		
		A	B	C
Low	)	6	4	2
	)	4	3	8
	)	8	2	1
		4	2	7
High	)	4	3	2
	)	2	1	4
	)	9	2	2
		7	2	2

(handwritten: 6, 3, 36/ 4.22, increase CI, great variance ↑ CI; 5, 2, 2.67, 3.22)

You are asked to state the following:

1. Average Range of experimental error, $\overline{R}$ 4

2. Standard Deviation, based on $\overline{R}$ ...... .591 ...... 2.364

3. Variance based on squared deviations 5.7778

4. Standard Deviation based on squared deviations 2.4037

Now, using only the last Standard Deviation, find:

	Temperatures	Heatings	Temp-Heat Combination
Standard Error Applicable	$\frac{2.4037}{\sqrt{9}}$ .801	$\frac{2.4037}{\sqrt{6}}$ .981	$\frac{2.4037}{\sqrt{3}}$ 1.39
Degrees Freedon (for q-Factor)	12	12	12
q-Factor	3.1	3.8	4.8
Confidence Interval	2.4831	3.7278	6.672

Show below which differences among the averages are significant:

(a) Differences between temparatures? Yes/No ...... No

(b) Differences between any two heats? Yes/No ...... No

(c) Any two individual cells? Yes/No ...... No

SUMMARY

Having acquired a set of tools for evaluating the significance of experimental outcomes, we have made good progress in becoming able to plan, design, perform and analyze experiments effectively and competently.

Obviously, however, there is more to be learned about the information contained in experimental outcomes. For example, we should be able to perform a full analysis of variances -- not just for the error term. Also, additional techniques of value can be added to our kit bag of useful and often crucial analysis methods. These will be covered in subsequent chapters.

Chapter IV

ANALYSIS OF VARIANCE

Once a properly designed and carefully executed experiment has been run, its evaluation involves (1) assessment of the experimental error, (2) graphing of the response data to help visualize the total pattern of relationship and emphasize meaningful trends, and (3) judging the significance of differences observed. A fourth step is the Analysis of Variance (Anova) in which the variances attributable to all experimental factors and their interactions are estimated.

Interaction

The term _interaction_ or _interaction effects_ is used with a specific meaning, to refer to the joint action of two experimental factors at different levels.

As an illustration, let us examine Figure IV-1, showing the effect of forming pressure (in pounds per square inch) in press working on the number of rejects, in percent, occurring. Two products,

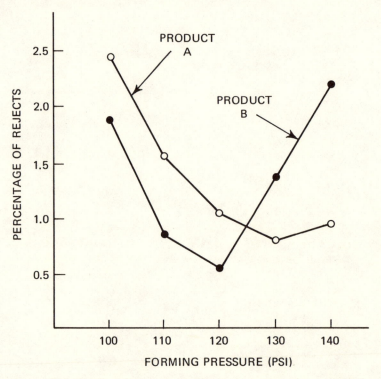

Figure IV-1: Typical interaction effects. Data represent result of investigation of rejects produced under various forming pressures for two products.

A and B, are produced on the forming press in this study. We note
that their trends do not run parallel, in fact, they cross. As a
result, while for Product A the optimal forming pressure is 130 psi,
for Product B it is 120. At first, from 100 to 120 pounds, the reject
levels do drop at approximately the same rate -- thus, parallel -- for
both products. Then, however, a differential action occurs. Product
B rejects rise sharply, while for A there is a continuing decline
followed by a moderate rise.

It is this inconsistency of effect of the levels of one factor
upon the levels of another that gives rise to what we call _interaction_.

Investigation of the causes of such differential effects often
leads to valuable clues for quality, cost or productivity improvements.
In the present example, it was found that the early rejects were the
result of inadequate pressure and consequent failure to attain required dimensional tolerances. Then, at higher pressures, the more intri-
cately structured Product B became especially susceptible to cracking
and chipping. Subsequently, a revision of heat treating of Product B
resulted in lowered brittleness and thus avoidance of cracking and
chipping under optimal forming pressures.

Curvilinear Effects

The data in Figure IV-1 are typical of most experimental outcomes.
The trend line is not straight. In this example the experiment has
encompassed a minimum point or "trough." In other applications involving a search for, say, strength a maximum point or "peak" may be
involved.

Although we have connected the data points with straight lines,
we realize that with a sufficient number of points a continuous curve
would have been the result. Sometimes people confuse a non-linear
relationship with "interaction." This type of error is understandable.
In many types of chemical processing, certain competing reactions among
ingredients, called "interaction" result in curvilinear effects. These
chemical interactions are of a different nature than statistical interactions.

Interaction and Error

Inconsistency of effects, resulting either in non-parallel or
crossing lines for the response data of an experiment, has been identified as statistical interaction. We must be careful, however, to
distinguish interaction from error. Some lack of parallel relations,
and occasionally even a cross-over, may be the result of experimental
error.

Examine the relations shown in Figure IV-2, for the yields from
our previous machine speeds and settings experiment. Then non-parallel trend of the averages for A and B, with A rising more sharply
than B, suggests the presence of some interaction. There is, however,
a relatively high range of variation of the test results associated
with each average, including some overlap (see right-hand part of

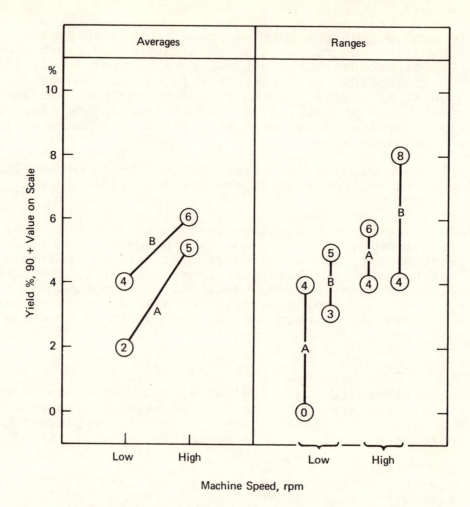

Figure IV-2: Yield from low and high machine speeds for machine settings A and B. The non-parallel trend of the averages suggests the presence of some interaction. However, there is a relatively high range of variation for each average with some overlap. Further statistical analysis will show experimental error, as revealed by the overlap of the ranges, to be so great as to make the observed interaction "not significant."

graph). Further statistical analysis, as will be demonstrated short-ly, will indicate that experimental error (implied and suggested by the overlap) is so great as to make the apparent interaction non-significant.

The overlap of the ranges, it should be emphasized, is shown merely to illustrate to the student how non-significance of the inter-actions is suggested by the nature of the data. Overlap does not necessarily mean absence of interaction. The only proper way to evaluate interaction and its significance is by means of the statis-tical calculations to be shown.

Variance Analysis Calculations

Not only the interaction, but also the so-called main-effects ascribable to the experimental factors, together with the experimental error, all can be evaluated in an overall scheme known as Analysis of Variance (Anova). We shall utilize as an illustration our familiar speed settings experiment.

Analysis of Variance begins with the various cell totals and factor totals of the original experimental units (or, in other words, the test results observed). These data are shown in schematic form in Figure IV-3.

Next, these totals are squared, summed and further analyzed as shown in Table IV-1, supplemented by the explanatory Table IV-2. The calculations are easier to perform than to explain. There is a good reason for the tabular arrangement of the data. When the reader gets ready to analyze his own experimental data, he will find the step-by-step procedures that run parallel for the various columns of factors, to be helpful.

Result of Calculations

Observe that we have obtained criteria for evaluating the significance of the main effects and the interaction, utilizing the experimental error Mean Square (which is also the error variance) as the denominator of the Mean Squares for factors and interaction. The latter are also a type of variance, but really a composite, which must be disentangled to obtain the net components as shown in Row k of the tabulation in Table IV-1.

By estimating the components of Variance, this analysis has gone beyond mere significance evaluation. Although these components are again estimates (of the true, but unknown universe Variances), they do give an indication of the relative magnitude of the various sources of variation that were operating during the experiment. Illustrated further in the form of a pie-chart (Figure IV-4), these components point to experimental error at 56% as by far the largest cause of overall variability, followed by speeds and settings at 33 and 11 percent respectively. Interaction effect, at a magnitude of zero, was absent and is omitted from the pie-chart. With the large amount of experimental error revealed, it is not surprising that speeds and settings did not show up as significant at the 95-percent confidence level.

When a factor has only two levels, such as Settings A and B, both the F-ratio (Table IV-1) and the previously given Confidence Interval (CI) give identical results. When more than 2 levels are involved, the F-ratio merely establishes whether or not there are significant differences among the levels, without identifying the individual pairs of averages. For the latter question, CI is needed. For example, assume that we had experimented with 3 settings, A, B and C giving average yields of 92, 94 and 98 respectively and a computed CI of 4.0. Then, we know that the differences between A and C and B and C, being 98-92 = 6 and 98-94 = 4 are significant (they equal or exceed the 4.0 of CI). On the other hand, between A and B the difference is only 2

ANALYSIS OF VARIANCE

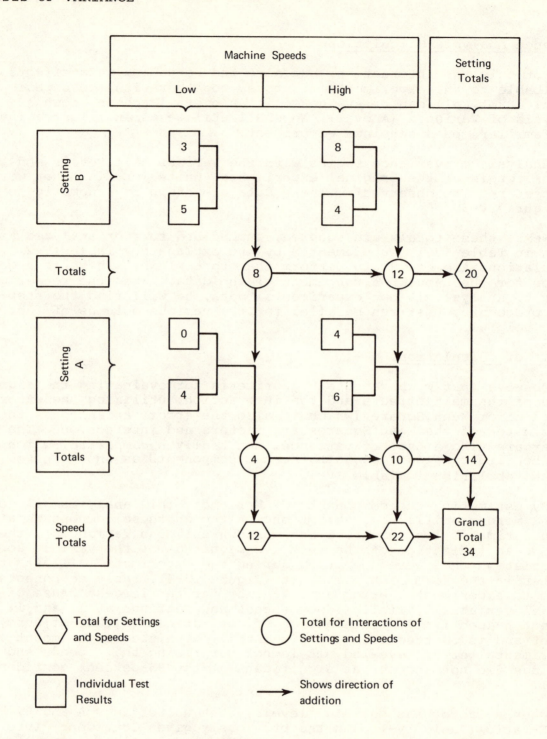

Figure IV-3: Effect of Machine Speeds and Settings on Yield (Percent — 90%). Data show how various totals are obtained for use in the Analysis of Variance calculations.

TABLE IV-1

ANALYSIS OF VARIANCE CALCULATIONS FOR SPEEDS-SETTINGS EXPERIMENT

Procedures	Sources of Variation				
	(1) Speeds	(2) Settings	(3) Interaction	(4) Error	(5) Total
a. Square the totals from Figure 3.	*low* 12^2 *high* 22^2	B 20^2 A 14^2	$8^2, 12^2$ $4^2, 10^2$		$3^2, 5^2, 4^2,$ $0^2, 8^2, 4^2,$ $4^2, 6^2$
b. Sum of a	628	596	324		182
c. No. of tests for each a total	4	4	2		1
d. b/c	157	149	162		182
e. $(34)^2/8 = C*$	144.5	144.5	144.5		144.5
f. Sum of Squares	$d_1 - C$ $= 12.5$	$d_2 - C$ $= 4.5$	$d_3 - C - f_1 - f_2$ $= 0.5$	$d_5 - d_3$ $= 20$	$d_5 - C$ $= 37.5$
g. Degrees Freedom *(no.of levels −1)*	$2 - 1 = 1$	$2 - 1 = 1$	$(2-1)(2-1)=1$	$4(2-1)=4$	$8-1=7$
h. Meansquare, f/g	12.5	4.5	0.5	5	-
i. F-ratio, h/h_4	2.5	0.9	0.1	-	-
i. F table ———→ $\frac{1}{4}$ 7.7		$\frac{1}{4}$ 7.7	$\frac{1}{4}$ 7.7		
j. Significance, %	nil	nil	nil	-	-
k. Component of Variance *prop due to speed setting interact*	$(h_1-h_3)/c_1$ $= 3$	$(h_2-h_3)/c_2$ $= 1$	$(h_3-h_4)/c_3$ $= 0**$	h_4 $= 5$	row total $= 9$
l. k as a % of k_5	33.3	11.1	0	55.6	100
m. Std. Dev., $\sqrt{k}$	1.7	1	0	2.2	3
n. Variation Coeff.***	1.8	1.1	0	2.3	3.2

*C = Correction Factor = (Grand Total of 34)^2/(No. of Tests = 8).

** A theoretical negative value results which is set equal to zero, the smallest actual amount of variation possible.

*** Standard Deviation expressed as a percent of the Grand Average 94.25.

TABLE IV-2
EXPLANATION OF VARIANCE ANALYSIS STEPS OF PRECEDING TABLE

(Rows a-n and columns 1-5 are identified. Thus "h_3" means row h, column 3.)

a. Enter and then square the totals shown in Figure IV-3.

b. Sum the squared totals, thus $12^2 + 22^2 = 144 + 484 = 628$.

c. Show how many individual tests comprise each total in a. Thus, for the first column, totals 12 and 22 each were obtained by adding 4 tests.

d. Perform the division. Thus, $628/4 = 157$. This is known as the "Crude Sum of Squares."

e. Find Factor C, which subtracted from d yields the "Sum of Squares," SS. The row cross-total must equal the total in column 5.

f. Obtain the "Sum of Squares" as shown.

g. Degrees of Freedom, DF for the error-term is found as previously shown. For the factors, subtract 1 from the level of each factor. Thus, since there were 2 levels of speed, DF = 2 - 1 = 1. Inter-action of two factors is found by multiplying the factor DF values. Thus, 1 x 1 = 1. For the total, note that there were 8 tests, so that DF = 8 - 1 = 7. Again, the row cross-total must equal the total in column 5.

h. Meansquares, MS are found from MS = SS/DF as shown.

i. Division of the error term into MS yields the F-ratio, which is then used to evaluate the significance of each source of varia-tion (columns 1-3) in terms of critical values of F, tabulated in the Appendix.

j. All F-ratios found are smaller than the critical values needed for significance. Speeds, setting and interaction are thus not significant at the 95% level.

k. From the MS, we can now estimate the individual Variance com-ponents by means of the formulas shown. Thus, $(h_1 - h_3)/c_1 = (12.5 - .5)/4 = 1.875.$ [3] The row total shows Total Variance. [1]

l. Variance components may also be shown as a proportion of Total Variance. Thus for speeds, $100 \times 1.875 / 7 = 26.8$ percent.
    33.3

m. The square root of each variance yields the well-known Standard Deviation σ. The row does not add up to total-σ, because the latter must be added vectorially, as in Figure IV-5.

n. Expressed as a percent of the Grand Average $(90 + 4.25 = 94.25)$, the Standard Deviation becomes the Variation Coefficient, V. Thus, $1.47/94.25 = 0.015$ or 1.5 percent for speeds.
    8   1.8

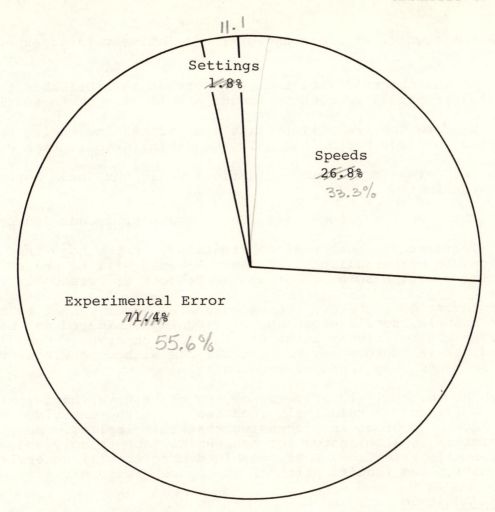

Figure IV-4: Pie chart showing relative contributions of variance components to total observed variance. Because of the relatively high experimental error, the effects of speeds and settings were not significant.

and therefore not significant. The F-ratio test would have merely indicated that there is at least one significant span between the averages of levels A, B and C.

Conclusions from Analysis

Let us see where we stand with the analysis of our speeds-settings experiments.

1. By graphing the averages, we noted that there is a tendency for higher machine speeds and for Setting B to give better yields. However, these effects as well as the interaction effect observed

are not significant, because of the relatively large experimental error term.

2. Of the observed variation, 56 percent is ascribable to experimental error, 33 percent to speeds and 11 percent to settings.

3. We have done relatively little experimenting, using only 2 levels for each factor and only the minimal replication of two.

The following further investigations would thus seem worthwhile considering:

1. Check on the effect of further levels of speeds and settings.

2. Increase the number of replications, in the hope that significance can be established. A lower F-ratio will be needed and Factor q will also be lower as the Degrees of Freedom increase.

3. Investigate whether the experimental error cannot be reduced. For example, some factors not previously considered may be producing the relatively large fluctuations observed. Once identified, these factors may be controllable with concomitant more uniform and thus improved processing.

Without the analysis of variance, we might never have realized the enormous magnitude -- relatively speaking -- of the experimental error and the lack of control in processing that this implies. But, once this variation is spotlighted for managerial, supervisory and engineering personnel's attention, their combined efforts will generally lead to recognition and rectification of the causes responsible.

Vectorial Addition

Variance components, as the example shows, add themselves in terms of squares. The process is akin to the well-known Pythagorean or vectorial addition, as further emphasized by the illustrative diagram in Figure IV-5.

ASSIGNMENT IV-1:

Utilize the data on coating weight in hundredths of a gram for the sheet-plating experiment, as reproduced below (but for simplicity subtracting 80 from each test result) to perform a full-fledged analysis of variance. The worksheet on page 66 will help in this task.

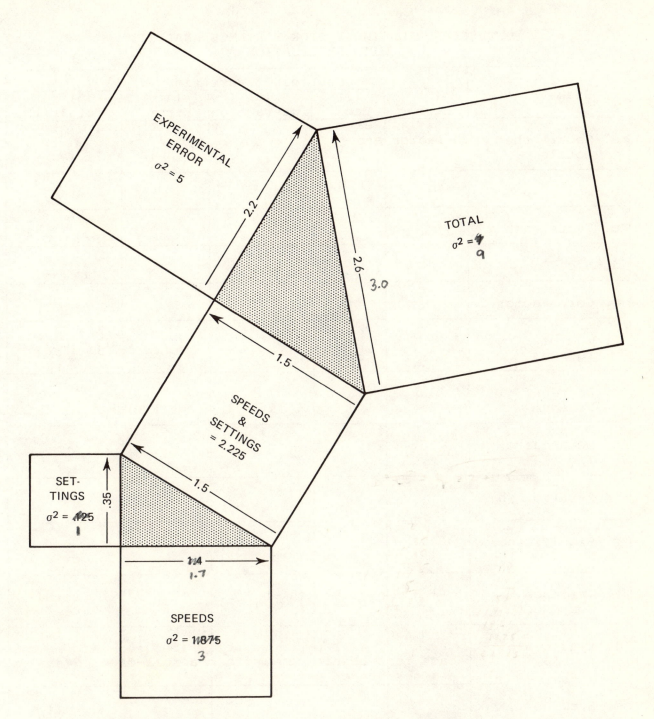

Figure IV-5: Vectorial addition of variance components yields total variance. The total Standard Deviation is thus $\sqrt{0.35+1.9+5} = 2.6$; or $\sqrt{2.25 + 5} = 2.6$.

ANALYSIS OF VARIANCE

WORKSHEET FOR TWO FACTOR VARIANCE ANALYSIS
WITH REPLICATION

Steps	Sources of Variation				
	(1) Strips	(2) Labs	(3) Interaction	(4) Error	(5) Total
a. Square the totals	8^2 16^2 18^2	24^2 8^2 10^2	4^2 8^2 12^2 2^2 2^2 4^2 2^2 6^2 2^2		1^2 3^2 1^2 1^2 2^2 1^2 2^2 6^2 1^2 1^2 4^2 2^2 7^2 5^2 3^2 1^2 1^2 1^2
b. Sum of a	644	740	292		162
c. Tests/each a	6	6	2		1
d. b/c	107.33	123.33	146		162
e. Corr.Factor, C	98	98	98		98
f. Sum of squares	$d_1 - C$ 9.33	$d_2 - C$ 25.33	$d_3 - C - f_1 f_2$ 13.34	16	$d_5 - C$ 64
g. Degrees Freedom	2	2	4	9	17
h. Meansquare, f/g	4.665	12.665	(3.335)	1.77	—
i. F-ratio, h/h_4 c_2 F-table	2.64 4.3	7.16 4.3	1.89 3.65	—	—
j. Significance, %	nil	yes	nil	—	—
k. Variance Component	$(h_1-h_3)/c_1$ .22	$(h_2-h_3)/c_2$ 1.555	$(h_3-h_4)/c_3$ .7825	h_4 1.77	row total: 4.34
l. k as a % of k_5	5.07%	35.94%	17.97%	41.01%	100
m. Std. Dev., $\sqrt{k}$	.47	1.25	.88	1.33	2.07
n. Var. Coeff.	.57	1.5	1.07	1.6	2.51

must add

must add

*

NOTES: Correction Factor, $C = (\text{Grand Total})^2/(\text{No. of Tests})$

$100 \times \dfrac{5}{GM}$

1 2 3 obsern — error large

Strip		Laboratory A	B	M	Strip Total	Grand Total	Grand Mean
1		1	1	1			
		3	1	1			
	Total	4	2	2	8		
2		2	1	4			
		6	1	2			
	Total	8	2	6	16		
3		7	3	1			
		5	1	1			
	Total	12	4	2	18		
Lab Total		24	8	10		4.2	2.33

82.33

The coding, involving subtraction of 80 from each observation, will not affect the calculation of the standard deviation. However, the grand mean above of 42/18 = 2.33 must now be corrected by restoring the 80, to yield Grand Mean = 82.33. Corresponding, the Variation Coefficient is 100 x (Standard Deviation) / 82.33. Recall also that the 82.33 is in terms of 100th of gram of coating.

Answer these questions now:

1. What do you now know about the two main effects and the error term?

    Effect of Strips: ___Is not significant___

    _____

    Effect of Laboratories: ___Is significant___

    _____

    Error Term: ___Almost 44% of observed variation___
    ___is attributed to experimental error.___

    What % variation due to factor 1, 2 interaction

2. What information is provided by the net components of
variance that was not previously available from either the Meansquares or the Confidence Interval analysis?

That a large portion of variance is attributable to experimental error.

3. Any other comments: _____

ASSIGNMENT IV-2: Variance Analysis Without Replications

Sometimes, as we have pointed out, it is not practically possible
to do replications. In order to illustrate Analysis without replications, let us assume for the Machine-Settings there had been only one
test per combination, and let us utilize the average of what are now
two tests. For example, Low Machine Speeds and Setting B had a replication, giving 3 and 5, with an average of 4; etc., so that we have:

	Machine Speeds		Totals
Settings	Low	High	
B	4	6	10
A	2	5	7
Totals	6	11	17

It is possible to use the worksheet on the next page, provided we
leave the column for "Interaction" empty (artifically assume that there
is no interaction, or that there is no separately determinable interaction).   Error is then estimated from the difference between the total
of column (5) and the effect of columns (1) + (2). Thus, in row "f",
column (4) use $f_5 - f_1 - f_2$, and in row k, columns (1) and (2) (use h_4
in place of h_3 for the calculation of Meansquares.)

Because this experiment had only 4 test values, the unusual result will occur that the Degrees of Freedom for the error term is DF =
1. Since tabulated values of the F-ratio often do not include a line
for this set, the following additional F- ratios will be needed in
order to assess significance of experimental results:

Degrees of Freedom for Denominator	Degrees of Freedom for Numerator					
	1	2	3	4	5	8
1	161	200	216	225	230	234

As you will surmise from the magnitude of these values, it is in
fact extremely difficult to establish significant results with DF = 1
in the error (denominator).

If DF are low → table is high because to allow for error

WORKSHEET FOR TWO FACTOR VARIANCE ANALYSIS
WITH REPLICATION

Steps	Sources of Variation				
	(1) Speeds	(2) Settings	(3) Error	(4)	(5) Total
a. Square the totals	6^2 11^2	10^2 7^2			4^2 6^2 2^2 5^2
b. Sum of a	157	149			81
c. Tests/each a	2	2			1
d. b/c	78.5	74.5		Interaction + Error	81
e. Corr.Factor,C	72.25	72.25			72.25
f. Sum of squares	$d_1 - C$ 6.25	$d_2 - C$ 2.25	$f_5 - f_1 - f_2$ .25		$d_5 - C$ 8.75
g. Degrees Freedom	$2-1=1$ 1	1	1		3
h. Meansquare, f/g	6.25	2.25	.25		—
i. F-ratio,h/h_4 F-table	25 161	9 161	—		—
j. Significance, %	nil	nil	—		—
k. Variance Component	$(h_1-h_3)/c_1$ 3	$(h_2-h_3)/c_2$ 1	h_3 .25		row total: 4.25
l. k as a % of k_5	70.6%	23.5%	5.9%		100
m. Std. Dev.,$\sqrt{k}$	1.7	1	.5		2.06
n. Var. Coeff.	1.8	1.06	.53		2.2

NOTES: Correction Factor, C = (Grand Total)^2/(No. of Tests)

variation explained by factor 1

could be like
5% error
.9% due to interact

ANALYSIS OF VARIANCE

After you have completed all this analysis work, you will discover that in place of leaving the Interaction column blank, you could have instead left the Error column blank; and that the Meansquare for Interaction so obtained is the same as the Meansquare you just found for Error.

This is not so contradictory as it may sound. In fact, when there are no replications, the interaction term merges into the error term and vice versa; or in plain English, error and interation are indistinguishable both practically and statistically.

ASSIGNMENT IV-3:

For further practice, it may be desirable to work a problem with 3 replications, such as given by the effects of forming pressure on hardness of industrial glass beads:

		Machine I	Machine II	Pressure Total
Low Pressure	)	2	3	
	)	2	5	
	)	2	4	
Total		6	12	18
High Pressure	)	4	6	
	)	8	4	
	)	6	5	
Total		18	15	33

1. Use the worksheet on the next page to perform the variance analysis calculations.

2. Discuss your results as regards:

a. Effect of pressures: _Significant_

b. Effect of machine type: _Not Significant_

c. Interactions: _Not Significant_

3. Make further observations that may be appropriate: _____

What appropriation of variance is due explained to machines, pressure intreaction, error

- 70 -

WORKSHEET FOR TWO FACTOR VARIANCE ANALYSIS WITH REPLICATION

Steps	Sources of Variation				
	(1) Machines	(2) Pressures	(3) Interaction	(4) Error	(5) Total
a. Square the totals	24^2 27^2	18^2 33^2	6^2 18^2 12^2 15^2		222354)^2 486645
b. Sum of a	1305	1413	729		255
c. Tests/each a	6	6	3		1
d. b/c	217.5	235.5	243		255
e. Corr.Factor, C	216.75	216.75	216.75		216.75
f. Sum of squares	$d_1 - c$ .75	$d_2 - c$ 18.75	$d_3-c-f_1-f_2$ 6.75	12	$d_5 - c$ 38.25
g. Degrees Freedom	1	1	1	8	11
h. Meansquare, f/g	.75	18.75	6.75	1.5	—
i. F-ratio, h/h_4 / F-table	.5 5.3	12.5 5.3	4.5 5.3	—	—
j. Significance, %	nil	Yes	nil	—	—
k. Variance Component	$(h_1-h_3)/c_1$ 0	$(h_2-h_3)/c_2$ 2	$(h_3-h_4)/c_3$ 1.75	h_4 1.5	row total: 5.25
l. k as a % of k_5	0	38.1%	33.34%	28.56	100
m. Std. Dev. $\sqrt{k}$	0	1.41	1.32	1.22	2.29
n. Var.Coeff.	0	33.18%	31.06%	28.71%	53.88%

NOTES: Correction Factor, C = (Grand Total)^2/(No. of Tests)

given diff set observations

ANALYSIS OF VARIANCE

One Factor Variance Analysis

When only one factor needs to be considered, the worksheets that have been provided can still be used, except that this time columns 2 and 3 are not filled out (consider them as containing zero entries in each space), because no second factor and thus also no interaction are involved.

An illustration of a one-factor analysis is taken from a welding application for two dissimilar steels. Because the weld had to with-stand high pressures, it was essential to achieve good physical, chemical and mechanical characteristics. Three different types of electrode composition, A, B and C were under consideration, and a number of pipes were welded with each. Care was taken to have clean surfaces, freedom from moisture and good support of the weld, as well as proper pre-heating and postweld heating, followed by heavy insulation to assure slow cooling rates. Subsequently, independent observers who did not know which electrode composition had been used, rated each weld (the lowest rating being 1, the highest 4). The results appear below:

Replication No.	Welding Electrode Composition		
	A	B	C
1	4	1	1
2	2	1	3
Total	6	2	4
Mean	3	1	2

We have thus a one-factor two-replicate experiment that appears to indicate that the best welds are obtainable from composition A, but a final judgment must await proper statistical analysis.

As a technical note, it may have occurred to those familiar with statistical methods of quality assurance that the data above could be analyzed by means of control charts. The Variance within each cell is the same regardless of whether we look at the problem as an Anova or a control-limit determination. Control chart analysis is indeed quite feasible*, although in many instances the Analysis of Variance permits a somewhat more sensitive evaluation.

In those instances in which only two levels are to be checked in a one-factor experiment, a special statistical technique known as the "t-test" may be applied, giving completely identical results to Anova. Because the t-test would be redundant, it is not used here.

---

*Usually, the average within-cell range serves to find the relevant process standard deviation.

ASSIGNMENT IV-4:

Using the worksheet on the next page, and omitting Columns 2 and 3 (enter 0 in each space, if you wish), perform the Anova steps needed for the electrode composition experiment. State your results:

1. Are the differences among compositions significant? __No__

2. What is the net component of variance
   due to compositions: __20.1%__

3. What is the error variance? __79.9%__

ASSIGNMENT IV-5: Review Problem

Glass containers for food and drinks are subject to cracking under the thermal shock of rapid temperature changes during washing and pasteurizing. Later, cracked bottles may break, causing costly losses in production when lines have to be stopped for the removal of glass and cleaning up of spilled contents. Worse yet, in rare instances a crack may remain hidden until the contents of a carbonated beverages or beer has been sealed under pressure, with subsequent explosion.

Assume that you have kept records of broken bottles in your plant, based on supplies received from 3 sources, A, B and C, for six months. The data appear below:

	Month	Supplier A	B	C	Monthly Total
WINTER	Jan.	3	8	10	21
	Feb.	5	7	8	20
	Mar.	3₁₁	4 ₁₉	10 ₂₈	17
	April	5	7	12	24
SPRING	May	0	2	10	12
	June	8	8	10 ₃₂	26
	Total	24 ¹³	36 ¹⁷	60	120

Using the worksheets provided, supply the following information:

1. Assuming the months to represent a replication of 6, so that there is a one-factor experiment, are the differences between the 3 suppliers significant at the 95 percent level? __Yes__

2. Give the following variances:
   Experimental Error __36.7%__ Suppliers __63.3%__

ANALYSIS OF VARIANCE

WORKSHEET FOR TWO FACTOR VARIANCE ANALYSIS WITH REPLICATION

Steps	Sources of Variation				
	(1) Electrodes	(2)	(3) Error	(4)	(5) Total
a. Square the totals	6^2 4^2 2^2				4 1 1 2 1 3
b. Sum of a	56				32
c. Tests/each a	2				1
d. b/c	28				32
e. Corr.Factor, C	24				24
f. Sum of squares	$d_1 - C$ 4		4		$d_5 - C$ 8
g. Degrees Freedom	2		3		5
h. Meansquare, f/g	2		1.33		—
i. F-ratio, h/h_4	1.5 9.6		—		—
j. Significance, %	nil		—		—
k. Variance Component	$(h_1-h_3)/c_1$ .335		h_3 1.33		row total: 1.665
l. k as a % of k_5	20.1%		79.9%		100%
m. Std. Dev., $\sqrt{k}$	.58		1.15		1.29
n. Var. Coeff.	29		57.5		64.5

NOTES: Correction Factor, $C = $ (Grand Total)^2/(No. of Tests)

WORKSHEET FOR TWO FACTOR VARIANCE ANALYSIS
WITH REPLICATION

Steps	Sources of Variation				
	(1) Suppliers	(2) Months	(3) Error	(4)	(5) Total
a. Square the totals	24^2 36^2 60^2				3 5 3 5 0 8 8 7 4 7 2 8 10 8 10 12 10 10
b. Sum of a	5472	2526			986
c. Tests/each a	6	3			1
d. b/c	912	842			986
e. Corr.Factor,C	800	800			800
f. Sum of squares	$d_1 - C$ 112	42	(32) 74		$d_5 - C$ 186
g. Degrees Freedom	2	5	(10) 15		17
h. Meansquare, f/g	56	8.4	(3.2) 4.93		—
i. F-ratio, h/h_4	(17.5) 11.36 (4.1) 3.7	(2.625) (3.3)	—		—
j. Significance, %	Yes	No	—		—
k. Variance Component	$(h_1-h_3)/c_1$ 8.5 (8.8)	1.73	(3.2)h_3 4.93		row total: 13.43 (13.73)
l. k as a % of k_5	(64.09) 63.3%	12.66	(23.30) 36.7%		100%
m. Std. Dev. $\sqrt{k}$	2.92	1.32	(1.79) 2.22		(3.71) 3.66
n. Var. Coeff.	(44.53%) 43.8	19.79	(26.84) 33.3		55.62 54.9

NOTES: Correction Factor, C = (Grand Total)^2/(No. of Tests)

ANALYSIS OF VARIANCE

WORKSHEET FOR TWO FACTOR VARIANCE ANALYSIS
WITH REPLICATION

Steps	Sources of Variation				
	(1) Suppliers	(2) Seasons	(3) Interaction	(4) Error	(5) Total
a. Square the totals	24^2 36^2 60^2	58^2 62^2	11^2 19^2 28^2 13^2 17^2 32^2		
b. Sum of a	5472	7208	2748		986
c. Tests/each a	6	9	3		1
d. b/c	912	800.9	916		986
e. Corr.Factor,C	800	800	800		800
f. Sum of squares	$d_1 - C$ 112	$d_2 - C$ .9	3.1	70	$d_5 - C$ 186
g. Degrees Freedom	2	1	2	12	17
h. Meansquare, f/g	56	.9	1.55	5.83	—
i. F-ratio,h/h_4	9.6 3.9	.15 4.7	.27 3.9	—	—
j. Significance, %	Yes	Nil	Nil	—	—
k. Variance Component	$(h_1-h_3)/c_1$ 9.075	$(h_2-h_3)/c_2$ 0	$(h_3-h_4)/c_3$ 0	h_4 5.83	row total: 14.905
l. k as a % of k_5	60.8%	0	0	39.2%	100%
m. Std. Dev.,$\sqrt{k}$	.95	0	0	2.41	3.86
n. Var. Coeff.	14.2	0	0	36.13	57.9

NOTES: Correction Factor, $C = (\text{Grand Total})^2/(\text{No. of Tests})$

3. Now, consider Months as a factor, perform a non-replicate experiment Anova.

    a. Are there significant differences between the months?

        _____ No _____

    b. What is the Experimental Error Variance? _____ 23.30% _____

4. Finally, consider the first 3 months as "Winter" and the next 3 as "Spring." The factor "Seasons" thus has 2 levels, each with a replication of 3 (the 3 months). For this 2-factor, 3-replicate experiment, determine the following:

    a. Seasons significant? _____ No _____

    b. Experimental Error Variance: _____ 39.2% _____

    c. Variance due to seasons: _____ 0 _____

    d. Interaction: _____ 0 _____

5. Discuss your findings, based on the analysis in No. 4, above.

Variance due to suppliers 60.8% _____

_____

_____

_____

_____

_____

SUMMARY

    In this chapter, we have presented the steps of Analysis of Variance. With this technique, we are able to take the outcome from a composite experiment and break it down into the various component factors -- their significance and the relative variation attributable to each. We will thus have squeezed the most from the experimental data.

Chapter V

MULTI-FACTOR INVESTIGATION

Mastery of the fundamentals of Variance Analysis, based on applications of one- and two-factor experiments, opens up to us many new roads to multi-factor studies and special factorial designs. This subject will now be discussed.

Three-Factor Analysis

An example will show the application of 3-factor analysis. The experiment was concerned with an investigation of shear strength in pounds of joints formed by ultrasonic welding. The factors studied were:

(a) Clamping force, at the levels of 140 and 160 pounds.

(b) Pulse time, at 1.0 and 1.5 seconds.

(c) Power, at 2400 and 2600 watts.

Instead of showing the actual levels, however, we may merely indicate them as plus or minus. Thus, heavy clamping force is +, light force is -; long and short pulse times are + and - respectively, and strong and weak current power are indicated similarly by + and -. The design of the experiment may be shown in cubic form as in Figure V-I. Using the letters a, b and c for Force, Time and Power respectively, we find that at "abc" all 3 factors were at the high level, while at the corner labeled "b" only Factor b was at the high level. Thus, the presence of any letter indicates the factor for which the level was high at that combination. At (1) all factors are at their low levels. In the center of the cube is a circled zero.

The shear strengths, in pounds, resulting from the experiment appear in Figure V-2. While this diagram aids in visualizing the nature of the experiments and its outcome, the customary form is that of tabular presentation, as in Table V-1.

Calculations

We are dealing with a 3-factor experiment, each factor at 2 levels, with a replication of 2 for each factor-level combination. Aside from the main effects represented by power, time and force, we must also expect interaction effects of power with time, power with force and time with force. There will also be a 3-way interaction of power with time and force combined. Finally, there remains the experimental error effect.

The calculation steps are parallel extensions of those previously shown for the simpler two-factor case, where only one interaction occurred. The data in Table V-1 provides the various totals needed to enter Row "a" of Table V-2.

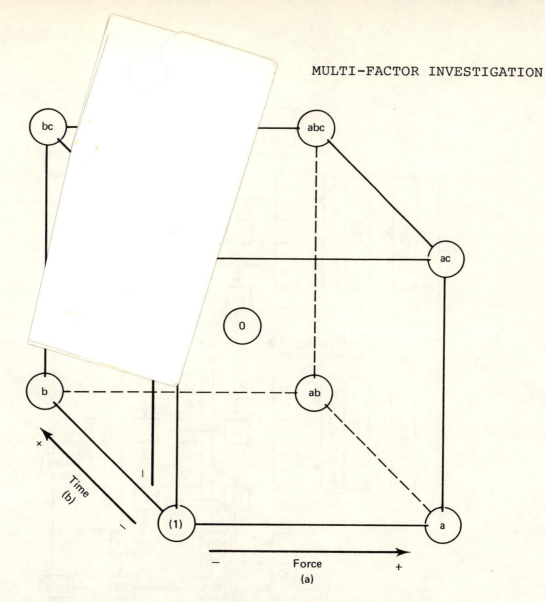

Figure V-I: Scheme of 3-factor, 2-level factorial, in three-dimensional visualization. Letters in circles show which factors are at the higher (+) level. At (1) all factors are at their lowest level. The point (0) is usually not determined in a factorial, but does indicate the center of the cube. It may be determined by means of a test with factors at midlevels (between + and −).

The detailed steps can be readily followed from this example. Using pencil and pad, the student should go through these calculations himself, observing how the variance components are developed. An examination of the F-ratios against a table of critical values (Appendix) will reveal all main effects and first-order interactions (that is P x T, P x F, and T x F) to be significant. The second-order interaction (also known as "3-way") of P x T x F is not significant and in fact is so small that it can be ignored.

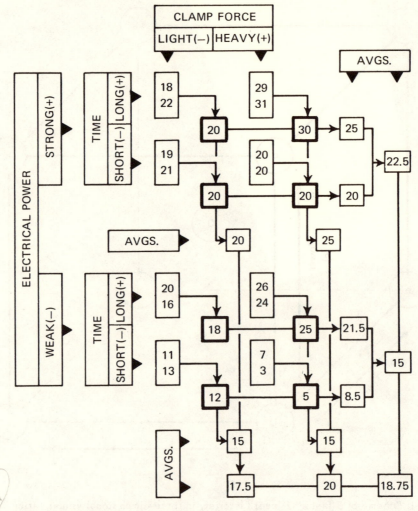

Figure V-2: Results of ultrasonic welding experiment. Data represent shear strengths in pounds.

Analysis of Findings

Analysis of the findings from a 3-factor experiment will be discussed by again referring to our illustrative case history of ultrasonic welding. As previously, we first graph the findings (Figure V-3).

We observe from Table V-2 a relatively large interaction of time with force. The Meansquare of 144 is more than twice as large as any other interaction, as is the Variance component of 35. This result is confirmed in Figure V-3. Looking at the two boxes for averages in the lower left and lower middle sections of the graph, we observe that at a light clamping force, there is very little difference in the effect of time on shear strength while at heavy clamping force, however, shear strength increases markedly with longer pulse. This differential nature of response between force and pulse has resulted in the considerable interaction variance of 35. On the other hand,

Table V-1: Ultrasonic Weld Shear Strengths

| Power | Time | Light Force | | | Heavy Force | | | Cross- |
		1	2	Total	1	2	Total	Total
Strong))	Long	18	22	40	29	31	60	100
)	Short	19	21	40	20	20	40	80
	Total			80			100	180
Weak)))	Long	20	16	36	26	24	50	86
	Short	11	13	24	7	3	10	34
	Total			60			60	120
Total[a]	Long	40	36	76	60	50	110	186
	Short	40	24	64	40	10	50	114
Total[b]				140			160	300[c]

[a]Combined for each of the two times separately, using the "strong" and "weak" power rows.

[b]Total for the "Total" row equals the row totals for "strong" and "weak" power above.

[c]Grand total, obtained by adding 140 + 160 in row or 180 + 120 in column.

NOTE: An independent check of the experimental error Variance can be obtained from the Average Variance among the replications (1) and (2). Since each Variance is based on only 2 test results, we apply a simplified formula, showing Average Variance σ^2 below

$$\frac{(18-22)^2 + (19-21)^2 + (29-31)^2 + \ldots + (7-3)^2}{16} = 4$$

where 16 is the total number of tests, and the Average Variance of 4 checks with the experimental error Variance of Table V-2.

(handwritten margin notes: "41", "4 factors = 24", "4 Factors = 24", "3 Factors = 4", "$3 \times 2 \times 1 + 1$")

Table V-2. Variance Analysis Calculations for Ultrasonic Welding Shear Strengths

	Factors			Interactions				(8) Error	(9) Total
	(1) Power, P	(2) Time, T	(3) Force, F	(4) PxT	(5) PxF	(6) TxF	(7) PxTxF		
a. Enter and then square the test totals	180^2 120^2	186^2 114^2	140^2 160^2	100^2 80^2 86^2 34	80^2 100^2 60^2 60^2	76^2 64^2 110^2 50^2	40^2 40^2 36 etc.*		18^2 22^2 19^2 etc.*
b. Sum of "a"	46,800	47,592	45,200	24,952	23,600	24,472	12,872		6468
c. Tests/each "a"	8	8	8	4	4	4	2		1
d. b/c	5850	5949	5650	6238	5900	6118	6436		6468
e. d − C**	225 e_1	324 e_2	25 e_3	613 $e_4-f_1-f_2$	275 $e_5-f_1-f_3$	493 $e_6-f_2-f_3$	811 e_7-f_1 to 6	d_9-d_7	843 e_9
f. Sum of Squares	=225	=324	=25	=64	=25	=144	=4	=32	=843
g. Degrees Freedom	2−1 =1	2−1 =1	2−1 =1	1x1 =1	1x1 =1	1x1 =1	1x1x1 =1	8(2−1) =8	16−1 =15
h. Meansquare, f/g	225	324	25	64	25	144	4	4	–
i. F-ratio, h/h8 (rounded)	h_1-h_8 56	h_2-h_8 81	h_3-h_8 6	h_4-h_8 16	h_5-h_8 6	h_6-h_8 36	h_7-h_8 1	h_8 –	–
j. Component of Variance (rounded)	c_1 =27.6	c_2 =40	c_3 =2.6	c_4 =15	c_5 =5	c_6 =35	c_7 =0	Row Total =4	Row Total 129.2

*For the 8 three-way interaction totals and the 16 individual test results respectively.

**Correction Factor, C = (Grand Total)²/(No. of Tests) = $(300)^2$/16 = 5625.

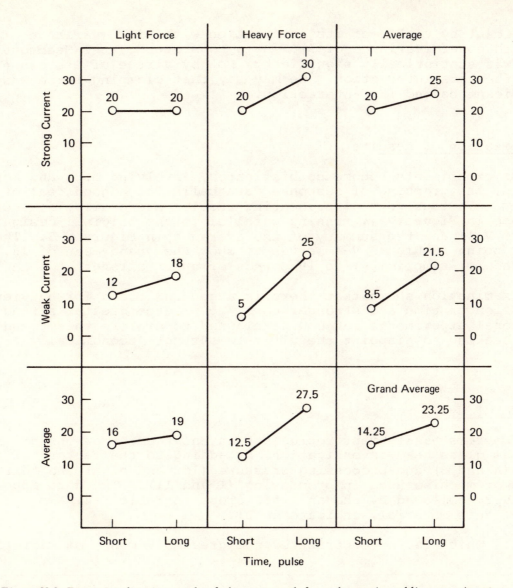

Figure V-3: Response data in pounds of shear strength from ultrasonic welding experiment, showing effect of clamping force (light and heavy), time (short and long pulse) and power supply (weak and strong current).

observation of the weak and strong current powers (upper right-hand and middle right-hand sections of graph) shows only a moderate differential effect with time, hence a relatively small interaction component of 15.

Among the 3 main effects, both time and power are important, with variances of 34 and 25 respectively. Clamping force, on the other hand, with a variance of zero is shown as having no effect <u>by itself</u> on shear strength. Yet, this clamping force factor did become significant by virtue of its interaction with time (variance of 35) and with power (variance of 5). As a consequence, the Meansquare for force was statistically significant, not by virtue of its own effect but rather its interaction. We may say that clamping force was not significant beyond its interaction.

Visualization of Results

As experiments become sophisticated, involving more and more factors, the graphing of response data calls for a good deal of ingenuity. Various ways of presenting results are available, such as the cube in Figure V-4, running parallel to the original design scheme (Figure V-1) and the summary of the averages in Figure V-5. The center point in Figure V-4 serves to show the grand mean of 18.75 (rounded for simplicity) to 19 pounds of shear strength.

Examination shows that there is a general trend for heavier force, longer time and stronger power to produce greater strengths. Additional experiments can now be planned to explore this trend further, seeking to pinpoint the ultimate strength economically attainable.

ASSIGNMENT V-1:

The first assignment represents an enlargement of our prior industrial glass bead investigation, by adding to the factors of supplier (A and B) and processing pressure (low and high) the third factor of machine used in processing (I and II). The data appear in Table V-3, followed by the analysis steps in Table V-4. From a review of this material, indicate next:

1. Which factor contributed the greatest amount of variation?

_____

_____

2. Which interactions proved significant at the 95 percent confidence level? _____

_____

3. Explain the meaning of the 3-way interaction?_____

_____

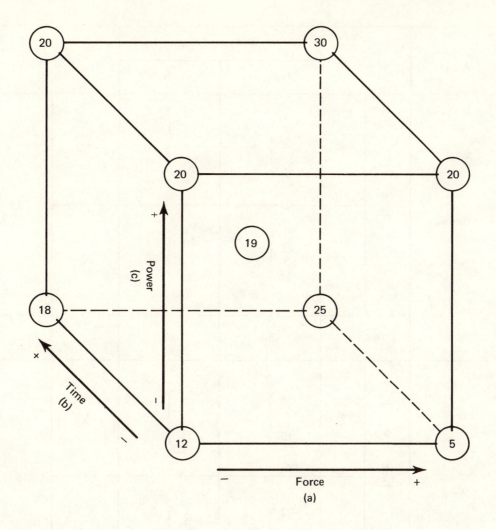

Figure V-4: Three-dimensional graphing of response from 3-factor, 2-level factorial. Response is shear strength in pounds. Center point is used to show Grand Average of the data, 19. The overall nature of the response can be obtained visually by studying this diagram and the response trends revealed.

Special Factorial Designs

Despite the valuable information content of full-fledged experiments involving many variables -- in practice, not just 3 but as many as 5, 6 and 7 variables may be involved in a factorial design -- there are always the considerations of materials costs, testing expenses and time pressures that place limitations on the scope of research and development investigations. Experimenters then have no choice but to resort to special approaches, even though the information so obtained may not be so complete as one might wish.

Among the most prominent factorials, to be discussed next, there are the Latin Square, the Graeco-Latin, and the Fractional Factorial.

Current Power			Clamping Force: Light, −	Clamping Force: Heavy, +	Average	
Strong, +	Time	Long, +	18, 22 } 20	29, 31 } 30	25	22.5
		Short, −	19, 21 } 20	20, 20 } 20	20	
	Average		20	25		
Weak, −	Time	Long, +	20, 16 } 18	26, 24 } 25	21.5	15
		Short, −	11, 13 } 12	7, 3 } 5	8.5	
	Average		15	15		
Average			17.5	20		18.75

Figure V-5: Shear strength from ultra-sonic welding, using 2 current powers, 2 pulse times, and 2 clamping forces, each replicated twice. Figures following brackets } are averages. Data coded for simplification.

Table V-3. Effect of Three Variables at Two Levels Each On Hardness of Glass Beads (In 100's of Knoop).

	Pressure	Supplier "A"				Supplier "B"				Cross Total
		Test 1	Test 2	Test 3	Total	Test 1	Test 2	Test 3	Total	
Machine I	Low	2	2	2	6	4	2	3	9	15
	High	4	8	6	18	5	5	5	15	33
	Total				24				24	48
Machine II	Low	3	5	4	12	7	3	5	15	27
	High	6	4	5	15	8	6	7	21	36
	Total				27				36	63
Machine I & II	Low	5	7	6	18	11	5	8	24	42
	High	10	12	11	33	13	11	12	36	69
	Total				51				60	111

Table V-4. Analysis of Variance

Procedures	Factors			Interactions					
	(1) Mach.	(2) Press.	(3) Supp.	(4) MxP	(5) SxP	(6) MxS	(7) MxPxS	(8) Error	(9) Total
a. Enter and square each number	48^2 63^2	42^2 69^2	51^2 60^2	15^2 33^2 27^2 36^2	18^2 33^2 24^2 36^2	24^2 24^2 27^2 36^2	$6^2, 18^2,$ $12^2, 15^2,$ $9^2, 15^2,$ $15^2, 21^2$		2^2 2^2 2^2 etc.
b. Sum of "a"	6273	6525	6201	3339	3285	3177	1701		591
c. Tests/each "a"	12	12	12	6	6	6	3		1
d. b/c	522.75	543.75	516.75	556.5	547.5	529.5	567.0		591
e. d–C*	9.37	30.37	3.37	43.12	34.12	16.12	53.62		77.62
f. Corrected sum of squares	e_1 $=9.37$	e_2 $=30.37$	e_3 $=3.37$	e_4-f_{1+2} $=3.38$	e_5-f_{2+3} $=-0.38$	e_6-f_{1+3} $=-3.38$	$e_7-f_1 \text{ to } 6$ $=3.37$	d_9-d_7 $=24$	e_9 $=77.62$
g. D. F.	1	1	1	1	1	1	1	16	23
h. Meansquare, f/g	9.37	30.37	3.37	3.38	0.38	3.38	3.37	1.5	3.37
j. Component of Variance	$\dfrac{h_1-j_4+6+8}{c_1}$ $=0.6036$	$\dfrac{h_2-j_4+5+8}{c_2}$ $=2.3797$	$\dfrac{h_3-j_5+6+8}{c_3}$ $=-0.1297$	$\dfrac{h_4-h_8}{c_4}$ $=0.3133$	$\dfrac{h_5-h_8}{c_5}$ $=0**$	$\dfrac{h_6-h_8}{c_6}$ $=0.3133$	$\dfrac{h_7-h_8}{c_7}$ $=0.6233$	h_8 $=1.5$	Row Total $=5.8629$
k. St. Dev. $\sqrt{j}$	0.78	1.54	0.36	0.56	0	0.56	0.79	1.22	2.42

M = Machines, P = Pressures, S = Suppliers.

*C = (Grand Total)^2/ (No. Tests) = $(111)^2/24$ = 513.88.

**Set negatives equal to zero.

Each of these designs represents certain short-cuts. Accordingly to the degree that full-fledged designs were not used, to that extent must one be guarded in drawing conclusions from the findings. Moreover, since our basic experimental outcomes are more tenuous in nature, we will often need to supply more refined and -- unfortunately -- more complex statistical analyses. Going back to the design state itself, the best avenues of approach in the short-cuts to be selected will require a considerable amount of thought, care and circumspection with the consequent demands on the judgment and ingenuity of engineers, managers and statisticians working together.

Although only a few reduced-experimentation approaches -- the predominant ones -- will be discussed, it should be understood that the number and variety of such specialized designs are large, and often one may have to improvise and invent new ones to fit the exigencies of a particular situation.

Latin Square

Usually, a Latin Square permits the evaluation of three experimental factors by doing only the amount of experimenting ordinarily required for a 2-factor design. This design, whose name has no particular significance, represents an experimental set-up in which the levels of the 3 factors under study have been arranged to form not only a square of equal numbers of columns and rows, but with the further provision that within the square cells are planned to contain only one level of the third factor within any column or row. Such a design represents a "square of n rows and n columns (thus n x n = n^2 cells), with each cell containing one of n levels of a further factor, each such level occurring once only in each row and column."

An illustration is given for the reliability improvement study in Figure V-6 of operator, torque setting and gasket material, each at 3 levels, and their effect on the rate of leaks per 1000 fastenings in the assembly of a pump. Loose as well as excessive tightening of bolts can cause leakage, the latter because undue tightness will distort the protective gasket. Accordingly, it was thought that torque setting of the pneumatic wrench when securing the bolts, type of gasket material used and operator skill would be the governing factors in leakage rates. Because of the considerable amount of time that must elapse before 1000 pumps are assembled and tested, a full-fledged factorial was out of the question. Even without replications, such an experiment involving 3 factors at 3 levels each would have involved 3 x 3 x 3 = 3^3 = 27 conditions. (With a replication of 2, there would have been 2 x 3^3 = 54 cells.) This fact may be visualized readily from a review of Figure V-6, by mentally replacing 3 gaskets A, B and C in place of the single gasket A or B or C in each of the 9 boxes.

Important in a Latin Square arrangement is the squaring-off in perfect balance of the third factor -- gaskets in our example. Thus, when the experiment has been run, each operator will have worked on each of the 3 gaskets. Similarly, each gasket will have been used in conjunction with each torque setting. The average of

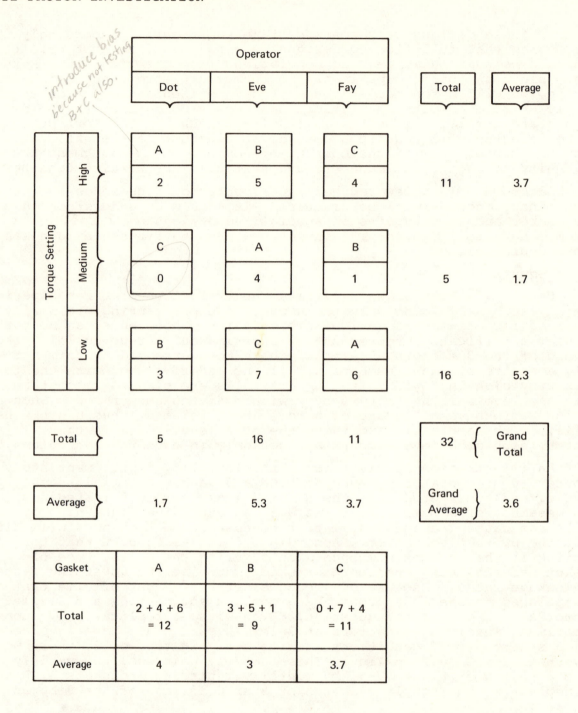

Figure V-6: Latin square design, illustrated from a reliability study. Effect of operator, torque setting and gasket material on number of leaks per 1000 fastenings.

1.7 leaks per 1000 fastenings for the medium-torque row, for example, includes the effect of each gasket (C, A and B) as well as each of the 3 operators (Dot, Eve and Faye).

test for main effects

Although we have balanced the experimental conditions, obtaining with only 9 conditions what would normally have required 27, our gain has involved a cost. In particular, we have lost the interaction effects of the factors. For example, to find interaction of gasket type with torque setting, we would need to know how gaskets A, B and C all used by one operator performed with each torque setting. Yet, take Operator Eve and Gasket B. We know how this gasket did at high torque setting -- there were 5 leaks per 1000 fastenings -- but we do not know how this gasket did at medium and low torques with Eve. The interaction effect is thus unknown. Even with replication, it would still remain unknown.

As regards the interaction variances, in a Latin Square only the 3-way interaction variance can be known, and that only when replications separate out the error variance. Without replications, the interaction variance merges into and thus becomes a part of the error term.

only find 3 way interaction, no 2 way interactions can be found

Evaluation of Latin Square

to get interaction ≥ 2

Steps leading to Meansquares, significances and variance components are self-explanatory from Table V-5. The procedures run parallel to those for ordinary factorials. Since in a Latin Square the number of levels per factor must always be the same for each, the factor Degrees of Freedom are all identical.

For our example, the error term is small (0.15 compared to a Meansquare of 0.75 for the smallest factor effect). We are thus assured of no important interactions. Had the error term been large, then we should have suspected high interactions. Nothing can then be done but to run additional experiments so as to fill out the open parts of the Latin Square (shown schematically in Figure V-7) until it is restored to a full factorial.

TORQUE	GASKET	OPERATOR		
		DOT	EVE	FAY
HIGH	A	2		
HIGH	B		5	
HIGH	C			4
MED	A		4	
MED	B			1
MED	C	0		
LOW	A			6
LOW	B	3		
LOW	C		7	

Figure V-7: Latin square design. Empty spaces indicate data points that would have been obtained with a corresponding full factorial.

no interaction separate because only one replication

Table V-5. Variance Analysis Calculations for Pump Reliability Study

(Leaks per 1000 Fastenings, Obtained with 3 Torque Wrench Settings, 3 Types of Gaskets and 3 Operators)

Procedures	Sources of Experimental Variation				
	(1) Settings	(2) Gaskets	(3) Operators	(4) Error	(5) Total
a. Enter and square the totals of the test results	11^2 5^2 16^2	12^2 9^2 11^2	5^2 16^2 11^2		2^2 $+5^2$ etc.*
b. Sum of squares in a	402	346	402		156
c. Tests per each total in a	3	3	3		1
d. Divide, b/c	134	115.3	134		156
e. Correction Factor, C**	113.8	113.8	113.8		113.8
f. Sum of Squares	$d_1 - C$ $=20.2$	$d_2 - C$ $=1.5$	$d_3 - C$ $=20.2$	$f_5 - f_3 - f_2 - f_1$ $=0.3$	$d_5 - C$ $=42.2$
g. Degrees of Freedom***	3-1=2	3-1=2	3-1=2	2	9-1=8
h. Meansquare, f/g	10.1	0.75	10.1	0.15	-
i. F-ratio, h/h_4	67	5	67	-	-
j. Significant?	Yes	No	Yes	-	-
k. Component of Variance	$(h_1 - h_4)/c_1$ $=3.32$	$(h_2 - h_4)/c_2$ $=0.2$	$(h_3 - h_4)/c_3$ $=3.32$	h_4 $=0.15$	Row Total $=6.99$
l. Standard Dev., $\sqrt{k}$	1.82	0.45	1.82	0.39	2.64

(handwritten: $\frac{2}{2}$ beside row i-settings; 19.0 under each F-ratio)

*For all of the 9 test results which are looked on as their "own totals" each.
**C = (Grand Total)^2/(No. of Tests) = $(32)^2/9$ = 113.8.
***For the 3 factors, DF = No. of Levels - 1 = 3 - 1 = 2 per factor. For total DF subtract 1 from the total number of tests. Experimental Error DF is found by subtraction of f_1, f_2 and f_3 from Total DF, thus 8 - 2 - 2 - 2 = 2.

We observe that gasket materials are unimportant, but settings and operators have a relatively sizeable variance and are quite significant. By reviewing the averages of Figure V-6, we conclude that a medium torque setting causes a significant reduction of leakage rates. Moreover, operator Dot achieves the best performance. We might investigate her special skill. Is there anything in her operating method that differs and results in superior reliability of the pumps as regards leakage? In the long run, considerable improvements and hopefully a "zero defects" situation may be accomplished.

ASSIGNMENT V-2:

Close control of the percentage of voids in asphaltic concrete will assure superior flexible pavements. In order to trace the sources of variation and their relative importance, the factors of melt temperature, binder mix fineness and spreading procedure were investigated. The resultant void percentages appear below:

| | Spreading Procedure | | | |
	A	B	C	Total
High Temperature:	F:2	M:1	C:1	4
Medium Temperature:	M:6	C:2	F:1	9
Low Temperature:	C:4	F:1	M:3	8
Total	12	4	5	

The letters F, M, and C stand for fine, medium and coarse binder mix. You are asked to perform the Latin Square analysis (work sheet on next page) and identify:

1. Greatest source of variation___Spread___.

2. Least source of variation___Temp.___.

Further Latin Square Designs

A 3-level Latin Square, as just illustrated, is often inadequate because of the fact that the error-term has only 2 Degrees of Freedom. As a result, unless the error-term is very small, it is hard to establish significance of any of the main effects observed. For this reason, it is desirable to have Latin Squares with at least 4 but preferably 5 levels of each factor. Usually, each factor must have the same number of levels, or else we cannot accomplish a full squaring and leveling off of the experimental combinations. There are however special designs, such as the so-called Youden Square, named after its inventor, which do permit some symmetry. The analysis then becomes complex.

A refinement on the Latin is the Graeco Latin Square, in which still another factor is included in the experiment. For example, assume that we had desired to include 3 types of bolts, a, b and c in the analysis. (Usually, Greek letters α, β, γ would be used.)

WORKSHEET FOR VARIANCE ANALYSIS
WITH REPLICATION

Steps	Sources of Variation				
	(1) Temperature	(2) Mix	(3) Spread	(4) Error	(5) Total
a. Square the totals	4^2 8^2 9^2	4^2 10^2 7^2	12^2 5^2 4^2		2,6,4,1 2,1,1,3 all x^2
b. Sum of a	161	165	185		73
c. Tests/each a	3	3	3		1
d. b/c	53.67	55	61.67		73
e. Corr.Factor,C	49	49	49		49
f. Sum of squares	$d_1 - C$ 4.67	$d_2 - C$ 6	$d_3 - C$ 12.67	.66	$d_5 - C$ 24
g. Degrees Freedom	2	2	2	2	8
h. Meansquare, f/g	2.335	3	6.335	.33	—
i. F-ratio, h/h_4	7.075	9.09	19.19	—	—
j. Significance, % table	No 19.0	No 19.0	Yes 19.0	—	—
k. Variance Component	$(h_1 - h_3)/c_1$ .67	$(h_2 - h_4)/c_2$ .89	$(h_3 - h_4)/c_3$ 2.0	h_4 .33	row total: 3.89
l. k as a % of k_5	17.22	22.88	51.41	8.49	100
m. Std. Dev., $\sqrt{k}$	.818	.94	1.414	.574	1.97
n. Var. Coeff.	35.10	40.34	60.69	24.64	84.55

NOTES: Correction Factor, $C = (\text{Grand Total})^2/(\text{No. of Tests})$

The Latin Square block in Figure V-6 would have been enlarged by providing also for this fourth factor as follows:

        Ac   Ba   Cb

        Ca   Ab   Bc

        Bb   Cc   Aa

Note that these 9 conditions take the place of $3^4 = 81$ tests of a full factorial. Unfortunately, for a 3-level Graeco-Latin design without replications, the experimental error term vanishes. There are no Degrees of Freedom left for it. Settings, gaskets, operators and bolts, at 2 degrees of freedom each, would consume all 8 of the degrees available. A minimum of 4 levels is therefore needed.

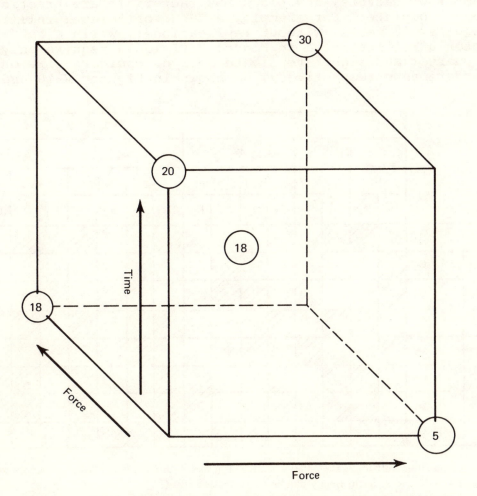

Figure V-8: Half-replicate 3-factor experiment at 2 levels. Of the 8 possible combinations for factors a, b and c, only 4 were tested, as shown by circles. Responses are inserted within each circle. The data correspond to those for the full factorial in Figure V-5, omitting those test results not provided by the fractional design. Note that the Grand Average (center point) differs because of the reduced test results available.

7 factor 7 levels
7⁷ combinations
& why use fract

Fractional Factorials

When it is desired not to use more than 2 levels at any factor, then resort to a fractional factorial will be useful. For example, a "half-replicate" factorial is one in which half the usual factor-level combinations are omitted. For a 3-factor experiment, the result would be as shown in Figure V-8. The missing corners can be estimated, but the estimate may be quite erroneous in the presence of strong interactions. Moreover, the evaluation of the factors and their significance becomes less precise.

On the other hand, when a large number of factors are evaluated, then the weight of the many points that are tested helps to overcome to a large extent the problems of estimation just mentioned. Upon further reflection, it will also become apparent that for a really large number of factors, any plans but factorials are practically impossible to complete. For example, a 7-factor 2-level full factorial would require 128 tests (without replications), while a half-replicate factorial (illustrated in Figure V-9) would require only 64 tests. Quarter and eighth-replicate designs would require only 32 and 16 experiments respectively, as shown in Figures V-10 and V-11.

			A_1								A_2						
			B_1				B_2				B_1				B_2		
			C_1		C_2		C_1		C_2		C_1		C_2		C_1		C_2	
			D_1	D_2	D_1	D_2	D_1	D_2	D_1	D_2	D_1	D_2	D_1	D_2	D_1	D_2	D_1	D_2
E_1	F_1	G_1																
		G_2																
	F_2	G_1																
		G_2																
E_2	F_1	G_1																
		G_2																
	F_2	G_1																
		G_2																

Figure V-9: Half-replicate 7-factor design. Factors A through G occur at two levels, subscripts 1 and 2, each. Empty blocks show omitted tests.

Interestingly, any Latin Square may also be viewed as a partially done 3-Factor, 3-levels-per-factor factorial; but fractional factorials usually involve only 2 (not 3) levels, or else even multiples of 2. Both the q-test and the F-test can be done on fractionals, but we still have the problem of estimating missing (purposely omitted) data points.

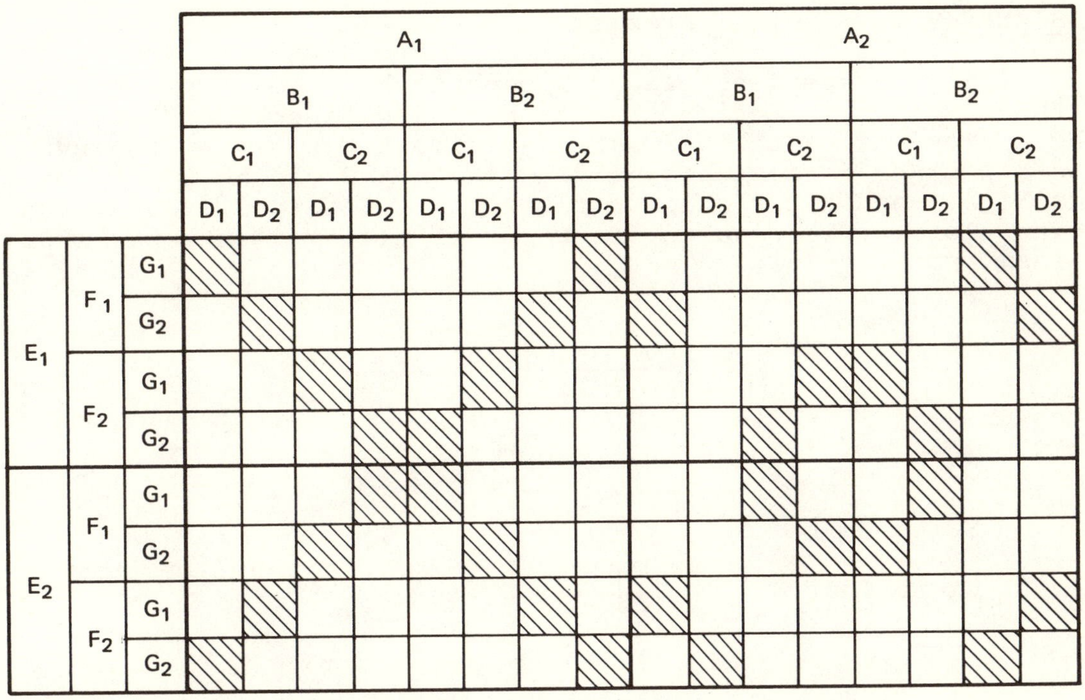

Figure V-10: Quarter-replicate design. Only 32 our of 128 tests are needed.

2×2×2×2×2×2×2

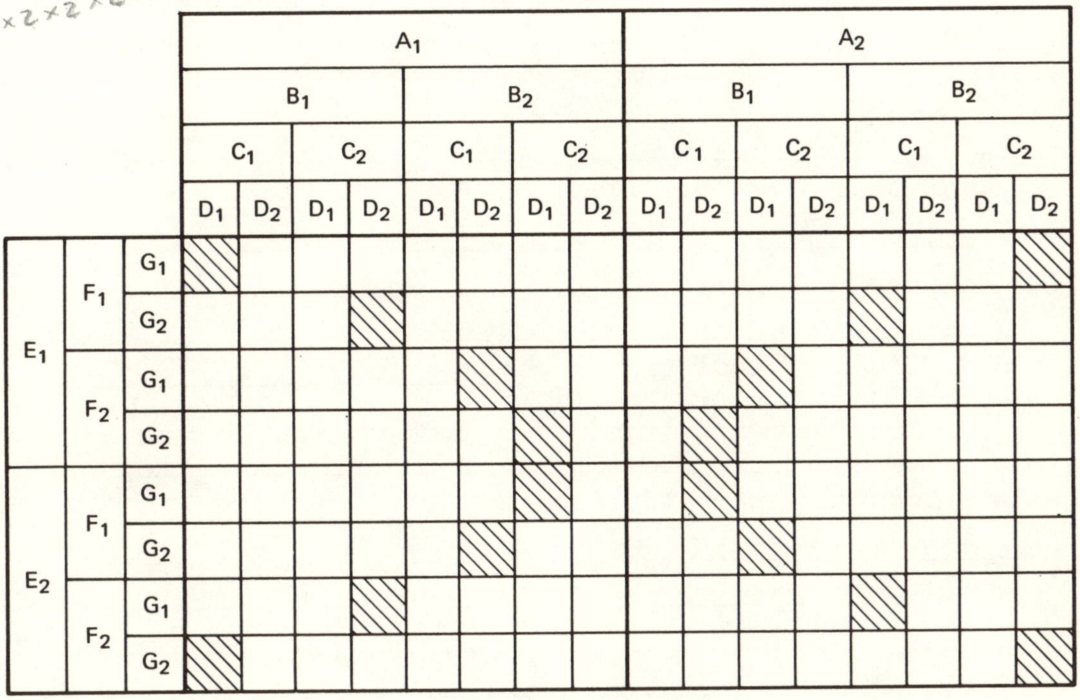

Figure V-11: Eighth-replicate design, using only 16 our of 128 possible tests.

MULTI-FACTOR INVESTIGATION

ASSIGNMENT V-3: Review Problem

A firm assembling electronic parts had been experiencing trouble with soldered connections in its products. Seeking the cause of these problems, a Latin Square experiment was set up to investigate the effect of three types of flux (A, B and C), the shift (Day, Swing and Night) and 3 tip-shapes of the soldering tool (round, square and triangular). The results, in terms of faulty joints per 1000 assemblies, appear below:

Type of Soldering Flux

	A	B	C	Total
Day Shift	(1)	[1]	△1	3
Swing Shift	△3	(0)	[0]	3
Night Shift	[2]	△2	(2)	6
Total	6	3	3	

The shapes drawn around each test result represent tool shape employed. You are asked to utilize the work-sheet on the next page to analyze the effects. Then state your findings below:

1. Effect of shift: _None_____

_____

2. Effect of solder flux: _None_____

_____

_____

3. Effect of tool tip shape: _None_____

_____

4. General recommendations:_____

_____

_____

_____

_____

WORKSHEET FOR VARIANCE ANALYSIS
WITH REPLICATION

Steps	Sources of Variation				
	(1) Shifts	(2) Tip	(3) Flux	(4) Error	(5) Total
a. Square the totals	$3^2\ 3^2\ 6^2$	$3^2\ 3^2\ 6^2$	$3^2\ 3^2\ 6^2$		111 300 222
b. Sum of a	54	54	54		24
c. Tests/each a	3	3	3		1
d. b/c	18	18	18		24
e. Corr. Factor, C	16	16	16		16
f. Sum of squares	$d_1 - C$ 2	$d_2 - C$ 2	$d_3 - C$ 2	2	$d_5 - C$ 8
g. Degrees Freedom	2	2	2	2	8
h. Meansquare, f/g	1	1	1	1	—
i. F-ratio, h/h_4	1	1	1	+	—
j. Significance, % Table	No 19.0	No 19.0	No 19.0	—	—
k. Variance Component	$(h_1-h_4)/c_1$ 0	$(h_2-h_4)/c_2$ 0	$(h_3-h_4)/c_3$ 0	h_4 1	row total: 1
l. k as a % of k_5	0	0	0	100	100
m. Std. Dev. $\sqrt{k}$	0	0	0	1	1
n. Var. Coeff.	0	0	0	75.19	75.19

NOTES: Correction Factor, C = (Grand Total)^2/(No. of Tests)

↑ Total Variance due to Error.

$\frac{1}{1} = 161$ Will not be significant

MULTI-FACTOR INVESTIGATION

ASSIGNMENT V-4: Further Review Problem

The data below indicate the effect on quality index of a super-alloy steel at various levels of amperage, cycling and vacuum pressure during processing.

Amperage	Operating Cycle	Light Vacuum Pressure			Heavy Vacuum Pressure			Cross-Total
		Test 1	Test 2	Total	Test 1	Test 2	Total	Total
High	Short	2	2	4	4	2	6	10
	Long	4	8	12	5	5	10	22
	Total			16			16	32
Low	Short	3	5	8	7	3	10	18
	Long	6	4	10	8	6	14	24
	Total			18			24	42
Total	Short	5	7	12	11	5	16	28
	Long	10	12	22	13	11	24	46
	Total			34			40	74*

* = Grand Total

Next, the data are plotted in Figure V-12, and the analysis of variance is shown in Table V-6.

Indicate below which of the factors and interactions are significant at the 95 percent level.

Factors:_____

_____

_____

Interactions:_____

_____

_____

Concluding Points

A variety of special adaptations and modifications of factorial experiments are possible. It was possible, in this chapter, to cover merely the highlights of these types of specialized designs.

When it is necessary to get a clear picture of the effects of each of a specific group of variables, no design is as good as the full factorial design. When it is not practicable to run a full factorial, then the special factorial designs achieve their objectives at the expense of confounding selected interactions and/or main effects with interaction. Naturally, the more measurements taken, the greater the resulting information and the greater the precision. In many cases, especially in industrial experiments, a loss in precision is

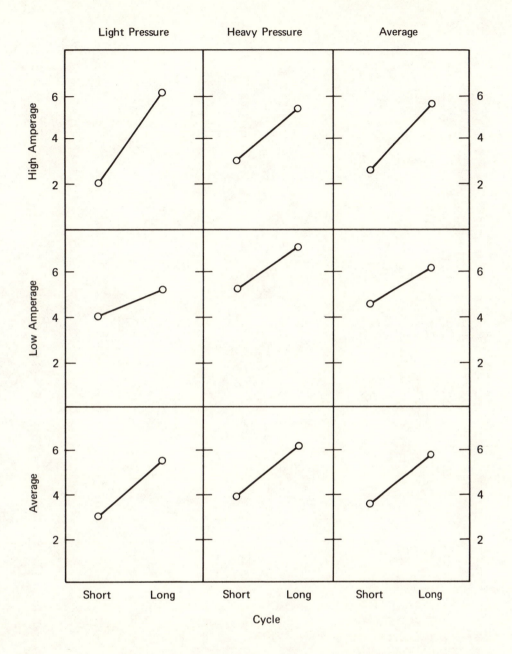

Figure V-12: Quality index points above 100 points, obtained in a consumable electrode vacuum melting experiment with two vacuum pressures (light and heavy), two operating cycles (short and long) and two amperages (high and low).

more than compensated for by the saving in time and expense.

You may feel that Analysis of Variance for experimentation has been discussed adequately enough. Nevertheless, there is a further group of Analysis of Variance techniques, applicable when data are in

Table V-6. Analysis of Variance Calculations

(A = Amperage, P = Vacuum Pressure, C = Operating Cycle)

Procedures	Factors (1) Amp.	(2) Cycle	(3) Press.	Interactions (4) AxC	(5) AxP	(6) CxP	(7) PxAxC	(8) Error	(9) Total
a. Enter and then square the test totals	$32^2,$ 42^2	28^2 46^2	34^2 40^2	10^2 22^2 18^2 24^2	16^2 16^2 18^2 24^2	12^2 22^2 16^2 24^2	$4^2, 6^2,$ $12^2, 10^2,$ $8^2, 10^2,$ $10^2, 14^2$		$2^2, 2^2,$ 4^2, etc.
b. Sum of "a"	2788	2900	2756	1484	1412	1460	756		402
c. Tests/each "a"	8	8	8	4	4	4	2		1
d. b/c	348.5	362.5	344.5	371.0	353.0	365.0	378		402
e. d−C*	6.25	20.25	2.25	28.75	10.75	22.75	35.75		59.75
f. Sum of Squares	e_1 $=6.25$	e_2 $=20.25$	e_3 $=2.25$	e_4-f_{1+2} $=2.25$	e_5-f_{1+3} $=2.25$	e_6-f_{2+3} $=0.25$	$e_7-f_{1 \text{ to } 6}$ $=2.25$	d_9-d_7 24	e_9 59.75
g. Degrees Freedom	1	1	1	1	1	1	1	8	15
h. Meansquare, f/g	6.25	20.25	2.25	2.25	2.25	0.25	2.25	3	—
i. F-ratio, h/h_8	2.08	6.75	0.75	0.75	0.75	0.08	0.75	—	—
j. Component of Variance	$\frac{h_1-h_8}{8}$ c_1 $=0.41$	$\frac{h_2-h_8}{8}$ c_2 $=2.16$	$\frac{h_3-h_8}{3}$ c_3 $=0$	$\frac{h_4-h_8}{8}$ c_4 0^{**}	$\frac{h_5-h_8}{8}$ c_5 0^{**}	$\frac{h_6-h_8}{8}$ c_6 0^{**}	$\frac{h_7-h_8}{8}$ c_7 0^{**}	h_8 $=3$	Row Total 5.57
k. St. Dev. $\sqrt{k}$	0.6	1.5					0	1.73	2.4

*Correction factor, C = (Grand Total)^2/(No. Tests) = $(74)^2$/16 = 342.25.

**Set negatives equal to zero.

a so-called "nested" or "hierarchial" form. Since the practical re-
searcher should recognize a nested form -- again, often an unavoidable design -- we will need a chapter also on this final major Analysis of Variace method.

Chapter VI

ANALYSIS OF NESTED EXPERIMENTS

Factorials generally are the most informative type of variance analysis, because the effect of the levels of each factor can be studied in combination with the levels of all other factors. For special and fractional factorials, this aim is only partially accomplished, but nevertheless selected levels can be investigated in combination. Occasions arise, however, when such a design is not feasible and resort must be had to a system known as a <u>nested</u> design.

Illustration

Our example comes from a process capability study on a pair of two-spindle automatics. Difficulties had been experienced in assembly because of excessive dimensional variations of a component produced by the two machines, A and B, in current production. Control charts had not revealed any dimensional difficulties.

While the actual investigation involved a good deal of sampling and measurements of the parts produced, our simplified data (in Figure VI-1) present merely the dimensional characteristics of four sample pieces from each spindle. A total of 16 test results is thus involved.

Nature of Nested Design

The nature of nesting will become apparent from a close study of the example. The <u>levels of one factor are nested within levels of another factor</u>. Here is how this nesting or sub-grouping occurs:

1. The factor Machines as two levels, A and B.

2. Under Level A, there is grouped and thus nested, the pair of levels 1A and 2A, pertaining to the factor Spindles.

3. Under Level B, Spindles 1B and 2B are similarly nested.

We can also call this arrangement "hierarchical," because the levels of the first factor, Machines, are built up in such a manner as to have the subsequent factors, Spindles, sub-grouped under each level. The classification Spindles is thus a sub-classification of Machines. For a further emphasis of the nature of nested arrangement, compare Figure VI-1 and the erroneous factorial design of Figure VI-2. The latter is erroneous because it would be improper to do the cross-totaling and cross-averaging shown.

The absence of factorial combinations means also that we cannot evaluate interactions.

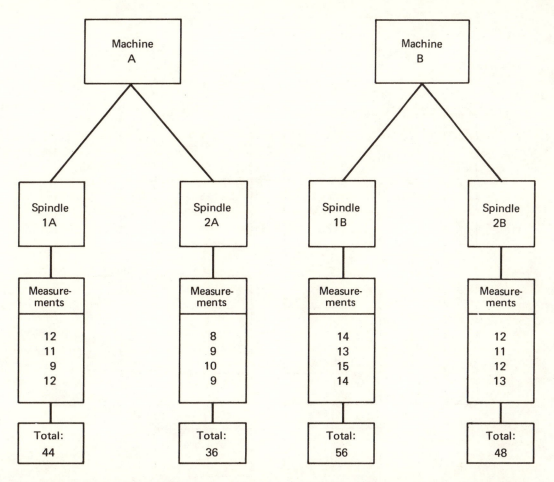

Figure VI-1: Process capability study. Abbreviated data, showing measurements of dimensions in 0.0001 inch plus 0.9990 inch. The illustration is a nested design in that each set of measurements, representing a replication of four, occurs grouped (or "nested") under one spindle only. Spindles 1 and 2 on each machine have been further labeled A and B to identify the machine and thus emphasize the fact that all four spindles are distinct. It would be incorrect to view the data above as representing a factorial arrangement.

The question may be raised: Cannot each spindle be removed from each machine and then interchanged between A and B? The answer is, no, not practically. In theory, we might succeed in making such an interchange, but in the process we would not be sure how well the spindles were re-attached, re-positioned and realigned after each switch. Moreover, and most importantly, such action would be fool-hardy by going counter to the objective of our study: to understand the relative variation of the factors Machines and Spindles in the actual production process. After all, we wish to know whether our process is capable of maintaining requisite uniformity of dimensions, not how well the set-up men can interchange spindles.

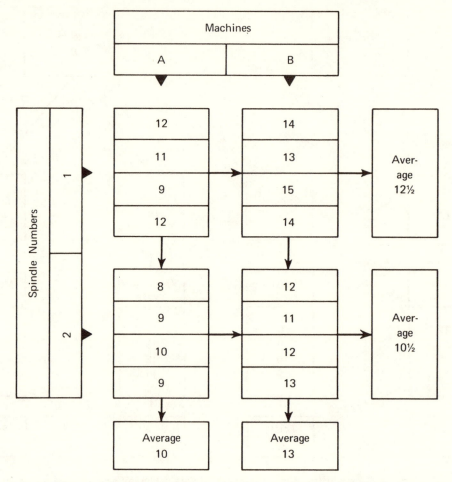

Figure VI-2: Factorial arrangement of process capability data. Incorrect method!
The factorial utilizes cross-totals and averages. This approach is not applicable
because Spindle No. 1 on Machine A is distinct from Spindle No. 1 on Machine B.
If, instead of Spindle Nos. 1 and 2, we have been studying a common factor, such
as two spindle speeds, 1 and 2, used equally on both machines, then the proper
arrangement is indeed a factorial, as shown above.

Calculations

For the actual analysis steps, the data are cast in suitable form
to obtain totals, as shown in Table VI-1. Next, proceed as shown in
Table VI-2. The calculations steps should be readily understandable,
and the following will be merely supplementary explanations:

1. Since there are two machines, A and B, the Degrees of Freedom for between-machine effects is 2 - 1 = 1.

Table VI-1. Process Capability Study on Two Machines
(Measurements of dimensions in 0.0001 inch plus 0.9990 inch)*

| | Machine A | | | Machine B | | | Machines A + B |
	Spindle No. 1A	Spindle No. 2A	Machine Total	Spindle No. 1B	Spindle No. 2B	Machine Total	Total
	12	8		14	12		
	11	9		13	11		
	9	10		15	12		
	12	9		14	13		
Total	44	36	80	56	48	104	184[a]

* For example, the entry of 12 signifies 0.9990 + 0.0012 = 1.0002 inch.

[a] A grand total for all 15 measurements.

Note that in a factorial, if Spindles 1A and 1B had been the same, we would have formed a new total; and similarly for 2A and 2B. Since the spindles are not the same, a nested design is involved, which must be analyzed accordingly.

---

2. Also, there are 2 spindles per machine. The D F per machine is thus 2-1 = 1. But there are 2 machines, so the total D F is 2 x (2-1) = 2.

3. Within spindle, there were 4 tests per spindle, thus 4- 1 = 3 degrees of freedom. But there were 4 spindles, so the total D F is 4 x (4-1) = 12.

4. Overall, with 16 total tests, there are 16 - 1 = 15 D F.

5. There is no separately identified error term. In evaluating between-spindle variations, the within-spindle Meansquare is used as error Variance. Similarly, for variation between machines, the "within machines" Variance becomes the corresponding error term.

6. More complete designations for within-machine and within-spindle Variance components would be "within machines but between spindles" and "within spindles but between tests."

The absence of a separately identifiable error team is characteristic of nested designs.

Evaluation of Results

Nested outcomes require greater analytical care than ordinary factorials, and it is often best to begin with an examination of the Variance components, as further highlighted in Figure VI-3. At a glance, between-machine variation shows up as the largest source of variation in current processing. At a magnitude of 3.5, it accounts for over half of total Variance. Reduction of this between-machine effect should be sought. Referring to the test results themselves,

Table VI-2. Variance Analysis for Process Capability Study
(Nested Experimental Design)

Calculation Steps	(1) Between Machines	(2) Within Machines	(3) Within Spindles	(4) Total
a. Square the test totals	80^2 104^2	44^2 36^2 56^2 48^2		$12^2, 8^2, 14^2, 12^2,$ $11^2, 9^2, 13^2, 11^2,$ $9^2, 10^2, 15^2, 12^2,$ $12^2, 9^2, 14^2, 13^2$
b. Sums of Step (a)	17,216	8672		2180
c. Number of tests comprising each entry of Step (a)	8	4		1
d. Step (b) $\div$ Step (c)	2152	2168		2180
e. Correction factor*	2116	2116		2116
f. Corrected sums of squares	$d_1 - e$ $= 36$	$d_2 - e - f_1$ $= 16$	$d_4 - d_2$ $= 12$	$d_4 - e$ $= 64$
g. Degrees of freedom**	$2 - 1 = 1$	$2(2-1) = 2$	$4(4-1) = 12$	$16 - 1 = 15$
h. Meansquares Step (f) $\div$ Step (g)	36	8	1	
i. F-ratios	$h_1 \div h_2$ $= 4.5$	$h_2 \div h_3$ $= 8$		
j. Significant at the 95% confidence level?	No	Yes		
k. Component of variance	$\dfrac{h_1 - h_2}{c_1}$ $= 3.5$	$\dfrac{h_2 - h_3}{c_2}$ $= 1.75$	h_3 $= 1.0$	$k_1 + k_2 + k_3$ $= 6.25$
l. Standard Deviations: $\sqrt{\text{Step (k)}}$	1.87	1.32	1.0	2.5

*Correction Factor, C, adjusts "Gross Sum of Squares" in "d" to Net Sum of Squares in "f". C = (Grand Total)^2/(Total No. of Measurements) = $(184)^2/16 = 2116$.

**For n = 2 machines, between-machine D F = n-1 = 2-1 = 1. For n = 2 spindles per each of the k = 2 machines, D F = k(n-1) = 2(2-1). For n = 4 measurements per each of the k = 4 spindles, D F k(n-1) = 12. For n = 16 tests in all, D F = n-1 = 16-1 = 15.

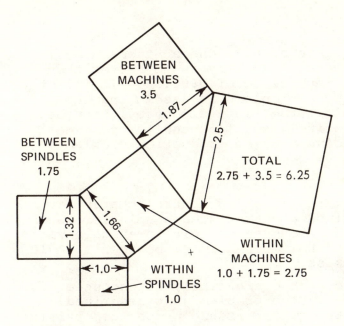

Figure VI-3: Sources of Variation. Spindle and machine effects on total variation, using data obtained from process capability study in a machining operation.

it is noted that Machine B produces on the average larger dimensions than A. An investigation of settings and other production factors is desirable, with the aim of standardizing the average level at which the two machines operate. Once both machines operate to practically the same average, then the between-machine variation will diminish.

There are also between-spindle differences, which at a variance of 1.75 are smaller than between-machine effects but certainly not negligible. Again, attention to minimizing the average level at which the two spindles on each machine work will reduce this component of variation.

Within-spindle variance is 1.0, and it was the judgment of those concerned that this could not be reduced without extensive overhaul and costly replacements of parts. Moreover, it was felt that once the between-machine and between-spindle differences had been minimized through proper attention to standardized settings and fixturing, the remaining variation would be quite tolerable.

Some students may be surprised that we have considered between-machine variation as the most important, even though it did not show up as statistically significant. The answer is that the F-ratio was not inconsiderable at 4.5, and it is practically impossible to obtain statistically satisfactory significance when the factor Degrees of Freedom is merely 1, and the error term D F is but 2. (The error term, as will be recalled, is obtained from the within-machine variation column for this nested design.) We are at the lowest D F corner of the F-ratio table (D F of 1 for numerator, D F of 2 for denominator) and an F-ratio of 18.5 or larger would be needed to establish significance. Nor could we have increased the Degrees of Freedom. There were just two machines and two spindles per machine, thus 2 x (2-1) = 2 Degrees of Freedom regardless of the number of tests per spindle (the equivalent of replication).

This evaluation also emphasizes the need for good judgment in analysis. Blind reliance on F-ratios and significance tests can be as misleading as failure to obtain these criteria in the first place.

ANALYSIS OF NESTED EXPERIMENTS

Process Capability

From the total processing variance of 6.25 and a Standard Deviation of 2.5, we note that the process capability is no better than ±3 x 2.5 = ±7.5, representing a maximum range of 0.0015*. It is not surprising, therefore, that there were problems in assembling such variable parts. Rectifications, along the lines discussed, brought about a quick improvement with relatively small expenditures. The statistical analysis thus helped solve a major production problem in short order.

Why the Control Chart Did Not Work

The example points up a major area in which control charts may fail a plant. The shop had maintained a chart on each spindle. Such a graph will indicate "no trouble" so long as the within-spindle variation is "in control," regardless of how much harmful between-spindle or between-machine variation may exist.

During routine production, shops that are likely to encounter the type of between-spindle or between-machine problem just described, should maintain group control charts. These assure proper supervision over the total process variability of groups of spindles or machines. Statistical analysis, such as shown, will usually point up the need for such charts.

A further point is worthy of note. The Analysis of Variance performed can be done readily without additional testing by merely utilizing the inspection records that result from the quality control work (and control charting) itself. This is not an unusual occurrence. Many times, needed data will be found to be available without special experiments.

ASSIGNMENT VI-1:

In order to understanding nested designs more fully, we may utilize our previous range-method of estimating Standard Deviation. Assuming that all measurements for each spindle occurred in random sequence, then the Range of dimensions for the four pieces per spindle represents within-spindle variation. Furthermore, a Range taken across the data (cross-range) represents the variation both within and among spindles and machines, thus overall variation. Obtain the ranges below:

Spindle Numbers				Range, R_O, Across
1A	2A	1B	2B	
12	8	14	12	6
11	9	13	11	4
9	10	15	12	6
12	9	14	13	5
Range within, R_W 3	2	2	2	

any row overall chang

each shows within spindles

---

*From the statistical characteristics of a Normal Curve, which generally is applicable for machining operations, a multiplication of the Standard Deviation by ±3 yields the upper and lower maximum of the production evaluated. Instead of saying ±7.5, we would also refer to a maximum range of just 2 x 7.5 = 15.

Now calculate the following:

	Within Spindles	Overall
1. Total Σ of Ranges, R_w and then R_o	9	21
2. Number, k, of Ranges, R_w and then R_o	4	4
3. Average Range, $\overline{R} = \Sigma R/k$	2.25	5.25
4. Sample Size, n, per each Range	4	4
5. Factor F_d (=$1/d_2$) from table (Appendix)	.486	.486
6. Standard Deviation, $\sigma = \overline{R} \times F_d$	1.09	2.55 — higher because other effects

Again we observe a considerable excess of overall compared to within-spindle variation, thus implying high between-spindle and between-machine effect.

ASSIGNMENT VI-2: Automotive Application of Nested Design

The following are records of impact strength tests on crankshafts produced at a foundry, with the resultant Charpy Impact Unnotched test results recorded in terms of foot-pounds:

Heat No. 101			Heat Totals
Mold No.6	Mold No.1	Mold No.8	
12	20	19	
20	19	20	
13	18	25	
17	16	26	
Totals 62	73	90	225

Heat No. 108			
Mold No.6	Mold No.7	Mold No.3	
17	29	16	
16	26	21	
17	22	15	
10	24	17	
Totals 60	101	69	230

ANALYSIS OF NESTED EXPERIMENTS

An Analysis of Variance yielded the results shown in Table VI-3. Examine the data, keeping in mind that a large customer has complained about an excessive amount of variation in the impact strengths of the crankshafts. Next, prepare this information-evaluation for plant management:

1. Heat-to-heat variation is _Not sign_____

_____

2. Mold-to-mold variation is _Significant_____

_____

_____

3. Variation between tests is _Quite large 33% variation____

_____

_____

4. Variation in future production may be reduced if the following factors of current variability are studied further from an engineering-research viewpoint: _____

_____

_____

_____

Also, why do you think you may have helped the plant take corrective action more quickly and economically than would have been likely without a statistical analysis of the data? _____

_____

_____

_____

_____

ASSIGNMENT VI-3: Review Problem

Reliability of automatically operated electro-mechanical connectors depends on the precision of response in terms of the uniformity of disconnecting force required. Aside from the possibility that too strong a connection might not separate when needed, or a weak connection might spring loose, unduly slow or fast acting connectors can cause instability, vibration and even jamming in the equipment affected. The company was especially interested in increasing the precision and thus upgrading the reliability of its K-293 connector, consisting of a plug with several pins and other corresponding sleeve-

Table VI-3. Solution For Automotive Example

	(1) Between Heats	(2) Between Molds Within Heats	(3) Between Test, Within Molds	(4) Total
a. Enter and square totals	225^2 230^2	62^2 73^2 etc.		12^2 20^2 etc.
b. Sum of "a"	103,525	35,835		9127
c. Tests/each "a"	12	4		1
d. b/c	8,627.08	8,958.75		9127
e. C*	8,626.04	8,626.04		8,626.04
f. Sum of squares	d_1-e $=1.04$	d_2-d_1 $=331.67$	d_4-d_2 $=168.25$	d_4-e $=500.96$
g. Degrees of freedom	$2-1=1$	$2(3-1)=4$	$6(4-1)=18$	$24-1=23$
h. Meansquare, f/g	1.04	82.92	9.35	21.78
i. F-ratios	h_1/h_2 $=.01$	h_2/h_3 $=8.87$		
j. Significant at 95%	no	yes		
k. Component of Variance	$\dfrac{h_1-h_2}{c_1}$ $=0**$	$\dfrac{h_2-h_3}{c_2}$ $=18.3925$	h_3 $=9.3472$	$k_1+k_2+k_3$ $=27.7397$
l. Standard Dev.	0	4.29	3.06	5.27
m. Variation coefficient, %	0	22.63	16.14	27.80

(handwritten annotation: d_2-C-f_1)

---

* C = (Grand Total)^2/(No. Tests) = $455^2/24$ = 8626.04.

** Set negatives equal to 0.

inserts in the receptacle. As a first step in this project, it was decided to study existing sources of variation in disconnecting force. From each of the three production lines, three connectors were sampled. Four tensile tests of disconnecting force, in pounds, were performed on each connector. The results appear below, supplemented by the analysis in Table VI-4.

Line No.		Test No.	Connector No.			Line Total
			1	2	3	
	)	1	1.6	1.9	2.2	
	)	2	1.3	1.6	1.9	
A	)	3	1.4	1.8	1.8	
	)	4	1.7	1.7	2.1	
		Total	6.0	7.0	8.0	21.0
	)	1	1.6	2.3	1.8	
	)	2	1.7	2.6	2.1	
B	)	3	1.9	2.7	1.9	
	)	4	1.8	2.4	2.2	
		Total	7.0	10.0	8.0	25.0
	)	1	2.4	1.7	1.6	
	)	2	2.2	1.8	1.7	
C	)	3	2.0	1.7	1.8	
	)	4	2.4	1.8	1.9	
		Total	9.0	7.0	7.0	23.0

Now comment on the following:

1. Are there any significant differences between assembly lines?

_____

2. Are there significant differences between connectors? _____

_____

3. Your recommendation is that the plant should _____

_____

_____

_____

Table VI-4. Variance Analysis for Disconnecting Force Data

Calculation Steps	Sources of Variation			
	(1) Between Lines	(2) Between Connectors Within Lines	(3) Within Connectors Between Test	(4) Total
a. Square the test totals	21^2 25^2 23^2	$6^2, 7^2, 9^2$ $7^2, 10^2, 7^2$ $8^2, 8^2, 7^2$		1.6^2 1.9^2 2.2^2 etc.*
b. Sum of Step (n)	1595	541		135.92
c. No. of tests comprising each entry in Step (a)	12	4		1
d. Step (b) $\div$ Step (c)	133	135		136
e. Correction Factor, $C = (\text{Grand Total})^2$ /Total tests $= (69)^2$ $\div 36 = 132$	132	132		132
f. Sums of squares	$d_1 - e = 1$	$d_2 - d_1 = 2$	$d_4 - d_2 = 1$	$d_4 - e = 4$
g. Degrees of freedom**	$3-1 = 2$	$3(3-1) = 6$	$9(4-1) = 27$	$36-1 = 35$
h. Mean squares Step (f) $\div$ Step (e)	0.50	0.33	0.04	
i. F-ratios,	$h_1 \div h_2 = 1.52$	$h_2 \div h_3 = 8.25$		
j. Significant at 95% confidence level?	No	Yes		
k. Component of variance	$(h_1 - h_2)/c_1$ $= 0.0142$	$(h_2 - h_3)/c_2$ 0.0725	h_3 0.04	$k_1 + k_2 + k_3$ 0.1267
l. Std. Dev., $\sqrt{k}$	0.12	0.27	0.20	0.36
m. Var. coeff., % $= (100 \times l)/\overline{\overline{X}}$***	6.3	14.1	10.4	18.8

* For all 36 individual test values.

** For the L = 3 lines, D.F. = L-1 = 3-1. For the C = 3 connectors in each of the 3 lines, D.F. = L(C-1) = 3(3-1). For the T = 4 tests per each of all the C = 9 connectors, D.F. – C(T-1) = 9(4-1). For all 36 individual tests, D.F. = 36-1.

*** Grand Average, $\overline{\overline{X}} = 1.92$.

ANALYSIS OF NESTED EXPERIMENTS

Summary

Nested data omit certain information, such as interaction effects, obtainable from factorials. Therefore we use it only in those
instances where factorials are inapplicable.

Despite these shortcomings, the results of an analysis of variance on nested data is likely to be quite valuable. The relative
variability of the various factors can be evaluated quite readily.
The research worker, design engineer, development engineer and project supervisor or plant foreman can use this information to good advantage in making processing improvements or worthwhile design re-
visions.

The objective of all types of analysis of variance work is
clear: Find the relative magnitude of various sources of variation!
Armed with this knowledge, further studies designed to hunt out and
eliminate undue sources of variation can be concentrated properly and
effectively on the most likely trouble spots in materials, products,
operations, designs or processing and related factors.

Chapter VII

EVOLUTIONARY PROCESS OPERATION

make improvements

Evolutionary Operation or EVOP for short, is a relatively new approach towards step-by-step improvement of a production process, until it reaches an optimum level in terms of quality, costs and yield.* EVOP is applied in current production by introducing at various intervals a series of systematic small changes in the levels at which various process variables are held. After each set of changes, the results - in terms of quality, cost, yield or other pertinent response - are reviewed. In turn, this review will result in further changes and evaluations, seeking through this gradual development to "nudge" the process into the best operating levels attainable.

Illustrative Example

Ingot production involved the use of three alloying elements, A, B and C, at nominal levels of 1.1, 1.6 and 0.8 percent respectively. It was desired to investigate whether small changes in these proportions would yield greater hot strength (in pounds per square inch, psi, times 10^3) than presently attained. A three factor experiment with two levels per factor, using current levels as the center point was designed as shown in Figure VII-1.

The EVOP setup is similar to a 3-factor 2-level factorial, with these modifications:

1. An experimental condition (0) is used, representing the center point of the levels of each factor. This point serves as a benchmark in evaluating the response from all EVOP trials.

2. Unlike laboratory experiments, which permit large changes in levels, EVOP requires small changes only. Otherwise, undue risks with regard to quality, yield or cost in actual production are taken. Yet, changes must be large enough so that an improvement will be observable from a limited number of trials.

3. When a phase of EVOP study has been completed, the preliminary optimum point discovered by this study becomes the new center point, from which to launch further EVOP investigations.

4. A particular line of EVOP research, such as the use of the three factors represented by elements A, B and C, will be discontinued when it is felt that maximum benefit has been attained.

---

*Developed by G.E.P. Box at Imperial Chemical Industries Ltd., and first published in "Applied Statistics", Vol. 6, No. 6, 1957.

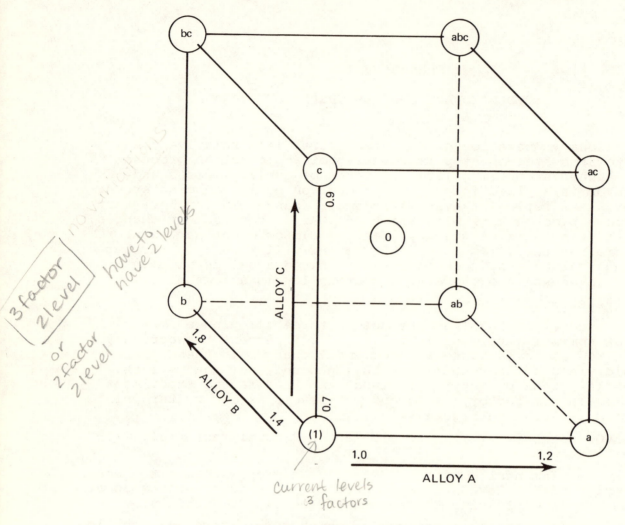

Figure VII-1. EVOP plan. The effects of 3 input variables, alloying elements A, B and C each at 2 levels of strength (proportion used) are evaluated in terms of the response variable of hot strength produced. Unlike a factorial the center point of the EVOP is used not to show the Grand Average, but rather the outcome when the center point of the levels of each factor is also studied. This serves as a benchmark in evaluating the response from all EVOP trials.

But new factors are then introduced, such as temperature or cooling cycles, stirring rate of the melt, and other variables considered of interest.

The philosophy of EVOP then is that a process should be run not only to produce product but also to yield information on how to improve it.

EVOP Steps

Our investigation of hot strength, in thousands of pounds per

Table VII-1: Steps Followed in a Four-Variables EVOP Program

Step	Procedure
1.	Select 3 input variables and 1 output variable. The output variable represents the response from the inputs.
2.	Plan the trial processing setups in accordance with a standard scheme, such as illustrated in Figure VII-1, using the standard designations of (1), "a", "b", etc., as indicated.
3.	Run a first EVOP cycle for each of the 9 trial setups, recording the results in a worksheet, such as in Figure VII-2.
4.	Run 2 further EVOP Cycles, making a total of 3 Cycles.
5.	Rank the test results for each Cycle. The best test result receives rank 1, the poorest, rank 9.
6.	Obtain the first rank sums, by totaling the 3 rankings under each setup.
7.	Compare the lowest rank sum with the critical rank value. If the sum is equal to or less than the critical value (Table of Critical Rank Values, Appendix), then we know at a 95 percent confidence level that the set-up represented by this lowest sum has yielded an optimum for the phase; and the phase is completed.
8.	If the lowest rank sum is above the critical rank value, at least one further Cycle is run, and a new set of rank sums is obtained, representing the total for each setup of all Cycles. Again the lowest rank sum is found and compared with the corresponding critical rank value.
9.	The procedures of Step 8 above are continued until the comparison of actual lowest rank sum with critical value indicates a significant lowest sum. The worksheet ends with 6 Cycles since, if no lowest sum is shown significant by that time, it is usually not worthwhile to continue the present line of investigation. If desired, however, one or two further Cycles may be run, yielding a total of 7 or 8 Cycles with corresponding Critical Rank Values of 16 and 20 respectively.
10.	If no significant lowest sum can be shown after 6, 7 and 8 Cycles, it generally means that the current phase of EVOP investigation is not leading to any practical lowest sum, thus suggesting that other processing variables be studied in further EVOP work.

Factors

A   B   C

1.0→1.2 1.4 → .7 →

Table VII-1, Continued

Step	Procedure
11.	When a significant lowest rank sum has been found, observe the arithmetic average of the test results for the set-up represented. If this average represents an improvement over prior processing results or prior EVOP phases, consider whether it should (a) be adopted for regular processing or (b) be used as merely a guide to further EVOP phases designed to discover still better set-ups and results. If the average found represents a decrease over prior processing results or EVOP phases, then review the matter: Should prior process set-ups, as regards variables under study be left alone? Is a prior EVOP phase leading to superior results? Should other levels of the variables be tried? In general, the making of decisions on what is or is not a real "improvement" and what levels and factors to study in EVOP investigations is a matter of engineering and related processing and product know-how.

NOTE: While 95 percent Confidence Levels are the ones most suitable for EVOP work, there is occasionally a desire to use 99 percent Confidence Levels. For this purpose, at least 4 Cycles are needed. The corresponding Critical Rank Values are 5, 7, 10, 13 and 16 for 4 to 8 Cycles respectively.

square inch, in ingot production serves to illustrate EVOP (Tables VII-1 and VII-2, Figures VII-2 and VII-3). The "processing setups" correspond to "treatments" or "factor-level combinations" while each cycle represents a replication.

The first phase used current operating practice (1.1, 1.6 and 0.8 percent for alloy ingredients A, B and C respectively) as the center point (0). After 4 cycles, the phase came to an optimum at Set-up "ac" with a strength of 44 (as against only 39 at the center point), representing a clear improvement. A further EVOP phase was decided on, using the "ac" setup as the center point. The phase required 5 cycles to come to a conclusion, and the phase-optimum again occurred at "ac". This time, however, hot strength was only 43, thus representing a slight loss against the prior optimum of 44. The EVOP Committee decided that the first phase had lead to an optimum that could not be improved by changes in the present variables under study. It was decided that other variables should now be studied, calling for an entirely new line of EVOP trials. It should be noted, however, that the Committee might have also chosen other courses, such as these:

1. Try some set-ups intermediate between those used in Phases 1 and 2; such as a center point of 1.15, 1.5 and 0.85 for A, B, C respectively.

2. Decide on other ingredient percentages, based on considerations of relative costs, thus seeking an optimum that does not necessarily lead to the strongest product but one that combines low cost with adequate strength.

Table VII-2: Four Variables EVOP Program. Illustration of Actual Use

Step	Procedure
1.	Input variables selected were alloy constituents A, B and C. Output variable was hot strength in psi x 10^3. Other output variables, such as elongation, hardness and other characteristics, can be included if desired.
2.	The results of the first 3 EVOP Cycles, in terms of strengths observed and corresponding rankings appear in the worksheet (Figure VII-2) for Phase 1. In Cycle I, for example, processing set-up "ac" gave the highest strength and is ranked first, while set-up "c" at a slightly lower strength is ranked second, and so on, for all 9 set-ups for each Cycle.
3.	For the first 3 Cycles, the sums of the ranks are found, with the lowest rank sum of 4 for setup "ac". This sum is greater than the critical rank sum of 3 (at left-hand side of row) needed for significance. Therefore, we must continue the EVOP phase with at least one further Cycle.
4.	The 4th Cycle is run and the ranks are recorded. The ranks for this Cycle are added to the ranks for the prior 3 Cycles. The resultant new lowest rank sum is 5, which satisfies the critical rank value of 6 for 4 Cycles. A significant lowest rank sum, at the 95 percent confidence level, has thus been demonstrated, and Phase 1 of the EVOP program is completed. The individual strengths obtained for "ac" in the four Cycles are 43, 43, 46 and 44, which average out to 44. This represents a considerable improvement over the prior processing set-ups shown by (0) of 38, 37, 42 and 39 averaging a strength of 39 in thousands of pounds per square inch. It may be possible, however, to attain still further improvements by additional phases. Normally, although not necessarily, the new center point (0) would be the optimum found from the immediately prior phase.
5.	A new Phase 2 is started. The new processing setups are centered about the last optimum of "ac" found from Step 4 above. Phase 2 went through 5 Cycles.
6.	The lowest rank sum is again at "ac", but averaging the strengths of 43, 43, 44, 45 and 40, we obtain only 43. This is below the 44 of the prior phase. The new phase thus has not resulted in any improvement. The slight decrease happens to be of little engineering significance.
7.	A decision must now be made. For example, Phase 2 may have overshot the optimum. A Phase 3 might investigate variables that are centered somewhere between the (0) set-ups of Phases 1 and 2. However, inasmuch as EVOP proceeds in small steps only, as regards changes in the levels of the variables under study, it may well be that Phase 1 did already yield the optimum of 44 for the particular variables (alloys) under study. Thus, it might be best to consider the current line of study complete, making such recommendations for processing changes as seem advisable from the EVOP results, and then considering other (new) variables to study in new lines of EVOP investigation on the processing equipment, settings, materials and operating procedures. Other types of alloys, temperatures, time factors, etc., may represent these new variables.

Full fledge factorial design

EVOLUTIONARY OPERATION									
Process Ingot Production			Phase 1			Date 6/1/66		By	
Study Hot Strength in Lb. per Square Inch × 10³									
Processing Setups									
Factors Studied	(1)	a	b	ab	c	ac	bc	abc	(0)
Alloy A, %	1.0	1.2	1.0	1.2	1.0	1.2	1.0	1.2	1.1
Alloy B, %	1.4	1.4	1.8	1.8	1.4	1.4	1.8	1.8	1.6
Alloy C, %	0.7	0.7	0.7	0.7	0.9	0.9	0.9	0.9	0.8

	Cycle	Test Results								
need at least 3 cycles to find significance	First	36	37	31	35	41	43	40	34	38
	Second	39	42	30	31	44	43	32	41	37
	Third	40	36	32	37	38	46	35	44	42
	Fourth	36	43	30	31	41	44	34	40	39
	Fifth									
	Sixth				Average:		44		Average:	39

		Ranking of Test Results								
Critical Rank Values 3	First	6	5	9	7	2	1	3	8	4
	Second	5	3	9	8	1	2	7	4	6
	Third	4	7	9	6	5	1	8	2	3
	Sum	15	15	27	21	8	4	18	14	13
6	Fourth	6	2	9	8	3	1	7	4	5
	Sum	21	17	36	29	11	⑤	25	18	18
9	Fifth									
	Sum									
12	Sixth									
	Sum									
Phase Optimum							✓			

if observed is < Rank → Then Sign

Figure VII-2. Illustration of an EVOP Worksheet

sign different from base
ac is sign diff → gives higher average strength

1.0 1.2 1.3
* Now use as midpoint

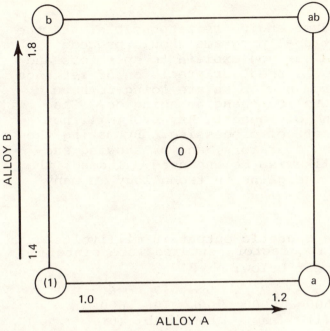

Figure VII-3: EVOP setup for 2 input variables.

Use of the sequential ranked sums for significance testing, as advocated for EVOP, represents a simplification of the more precise methods of Analysis of Variance. Such a simplification appears justified, however, from a viewpoint of convenience of application on the production floor.

The illustration given involved 3 input variables and one output or response variable. However, several response variables might have been recorded simultaneously, such as not only strength but also elongation and hardness. For 2 in place of 3 input variables, the setup of Figure VII-3 would be applicable. The worksheet can still be used, but with these alterations:

1. Setups c, ac, bc and abc are omitted. We have no trials and no response values for these 4 points.

2. From the Table (Appendix) of Critical Rank Values values for a two-input-variables EVOP are applied. For a 95 percent confidence level, therefore, values 3, 5, 7 and 9 replace 3, 6, 9 and 12 for 3, 4, 5 and 6 cycles respectively.

Special Feature

A special feature of the sequential ranked sums is that in those instances where there are marked effects from the EVOP application, only 3 Cycles are likely to be needed. If, occasionally, it is necessary to use as many as 6 or 8 Cycles, this indicates that the differences among the effects are relatively small and require this additional evidence in order to show significance. It seems hardly warranted to go beyond 8 Cycles in any EVOP phase. If significance cannot be established by the time 6, 7 or 8 Cycles have been run -- and the decision of where to make the particular cut-off is dependent upon individual conditions -- then it is usually not worth the extra time and effort to try further along current lines. Instead, new investigations along new lines would be more promising.

Caution

A word of caution is needed. EVOP is applied to current production. Greater care is needed, therefore, than in laboratory-scale investigations. Errors will not only affect production, but may have further repercussions on morale in general. Wise management will provide for representation of all important people on an EVOP team: the foreman concerned, process and product engineers responsible, and the quality control department. Educational programs should precede actual EVOP applications. How else can you explain to operators and foremen, who have been imbued with the need for precision of settings and processing adjustments, that from now on we are going to have a great deal of changing, albeit controlled changing going on? Case histories show that by proper laying of foundations, EVOP will not only improve the technological aspects of processing. By making the job more interesting for foremen and operators, and by showing successful improvements, morale will likewise be enhanced. Indeed, the effect on the people far outweighs the gains in technology in many plants.

ASSIGNMENT VII-1:

It was desired to increase the magnetic output in millivolts of a core used in memory circuits. The two factors studied were sintering time and temperature. The data appear below:

A - Time, minutes:	5	7	5	7	6
B - Temperature, ^{O}C:	500	500	700	700	600
Designation:	(1)	a	b	ab	(0)

Test Results after each
Cycle; in millivolts

Cycle I:	25	26	28	22	20
Rank:	3	2	1	4	5
Cycle II:	22	25	23	22	21
Rank:	3.5	1	2	3.5	5
Cycle III:	30	29	25	26	24
Rank:	1	2	4	3	5
Cycle IV:	19	20	21	18	22
Rank:	4	3	2	5	1
Cycle V:	17	18	24	19	16
Rank:	4	3	1	2	5

Required:

1. Show the ranking for at least the first 3 Cycles, inserting the values found in the spaces provided above.

draw backs
Phase I + II

∝. 3 way tie 4 4 4

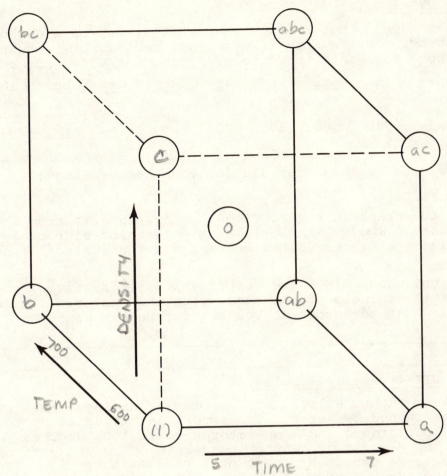

Figure VII-4: EVOP cube for use in entering variables. (See Assignment VII-3).

2. Next, determine whether or not you have reached an endpoint.
Yes:_____ No:____✓____ (Use Appendix Table of Critical Rank Values).

3. If the answer to No. 2 was "no" continue your analysis.

4. When you come to a stop, indicate the optimum found._No opt found_

5. What further study would you recommend for the next EVOP phase?

_More Cycles_____

_____

(Your reply should include your reasons).

EVOLUTIONARY PROCESS OPERATION

✳ ASSIGNMENT VII-2:

For the core output EVOP, assume that it has been decided to add another factor, core density in grams per centimeter, ranging from 3.00 to 3.06. How would the date of Assignment VII-2 now be enlarged?

Designation:	(1)	a	b	ab	c	ac	bc	abc	(0)
Time, min.	5	7	5	7	5	7	5	7	6
Temperature	500	500	700	700	500	500	700	700	600
Density	3.0	3.0	3.0	3.0	3.06	3.06	3.06	3.06	3.03

Complete the spaces provided for your answer, above.

✳ ASSIGNMENT VII-3:

Using the graph in Figure VII-4, enter the data from the assignment immediately above. Employ the base line for sintering time, the diagonal line for sintering temperature and the vertical line for density.

Later on, when all of the test results are received, the averages for each of the corners of the cube, plus the center of the cube, can be entered. What advantage do you see for such a procedure? _____

_____

_____

✳ ASSIGNMENT VII-4: Review Problem

High temperature alloys, for use in jet engines, must withstand the stresses caused by jet turbine rotors revolving at up to 30,000 revolutions per minute and temperatures up to 1600 degrees Fahrenheit. Because of the newness of many processes, such as production in consumable electrode vacuum arc melting furnaces, there is a lack of complete knowledge of the effects of all variables. The following represents highly simplified data on three cycles of EVOP experimentation on a super alloy steel. The data are in terms of quality index points above the Index of 100, considered to represent minimum standards of safety and acceptability for this steel.

FACTOR A   FACTOR B   FACTOR C   FACTOR C

Amperage	Furnace Operation	Light Vacuum Pressure Cycle (1)	Cycle (2)	Cycle (3)	Total	Heavy Vacuum Pressure Cycle (1)	Cycle (2)	Cycle (3)	Total
High	Short	1	4	1	6	1	2	1	4
High	Long	3	3	3	9	2	5	2	9
Low	Short	4	6	2	12	7	4	4	15
Low	Long	5	8	5	18	6	3	3	12

3 cycles

EVOLUTIONARY OPERATION									
Process			Phase		Date		By		
Study									

Factors Studied	Setups								
	(1)	a	b	ab	c	ac	bc	abc	(0)
A Amp	LOW	HI	LO	HI	LO	HI	LO	HI	MED
B furn	SH	SH	LO	LO	SH	SH	LO	LO	MED
C Press	LI	LI	LI	LI	HE	HE	HE	HE	MED

	Cycle	Test Results								
	1st	4	1	5	3	7	1	6	2	4
	2nd	6	4	8	3	4	2	3	5	3
	3rd	2	1	5	3	4	1	3	2	5
	4th									
	5th									
	6th									

		Ranking of Test Results								
Critical Rank Values	1st	5.5	1.5	7	4	9	1.5	8	3	5.5
	2nd		5.5	1	7.5	5.5	1	7.5		1
3	3rd	6.5	8.5	1	5.5	2	1.5		10.5	
	Sum	12.5	12.5	5	17	8.5	4		13.5	17
6	4th									
	Sum									
9	5th									
	Sum									
12	6th									
	Sum									
Phase Optimum										

Figure VII-5. Worksheet for Assignment VII-4.

no significance

Run more cycles

EVOLUTIONARY PROCESS OPERATION

For the center point, the three successive Cycles yielded 4, 3 and 5 respectively.

Next, proceed as follows:

1. Enter the Cycle results on the worksheet provided (Figure VII-5).

(Note that in some instances you may have problems of a tie in ranking, because two (or more) test results in a Cycle may have the same value. In such instances, split the ranking. Thus, if 2 tests results would both vie for Rank 4, then call them both 4-1/2. The next test result is ranked as 6 (not 5), since the 2 values of 4-1/2 take the place of both 4 and 5.)

2. If there is an optimum, state this here: _____

_____

_____

_____

Summary

Although similar to factorials, EVOP applications are considered a distinct approach, because they are tailored for employment during production. EVOP philosophy is that a process should not merely yield output, but also information on how to improve the quality, reliability, productivity and cost aspects of production.

Because EVOP is used during production, often by production people who may not have time to consult a statistician on decisions of a routine nature, various short-cuts have been devised. The original shortcuts, developed by the inventor of EVOP, Dr. G.E.P. Box (at Imperial Chemical Industries) used ranges*, the still simpler approach given here employs critical rank sums**.

The value of EVOP is not merely that it provides important, valuable process information. Experience has shown that where production engineers, supervisors and foremen utilize EVOP, they develop new insights and interests in the production process and their work as a whole. Improved morale, stimulated by a search for continued improvements, is thus often a significant by-product.

---

*For an example of application of ranges, see the Chapter on Evolutionary Operation in Enrick, N.L. "Quality Control and Reliability" 7th ed., Industrial Press, New York, N.Y. 10157.

**The concept of critical rank values originated with Dr. Marvin Zelen, Experimental Statistics Section, National Cancer Institute, Bethesda, Maryland. The critical rank values provided in this Workbook were computed by N.L. Enrick (representing extensions of the original values by Dr. Zelen).

(handwritten top margin)
regression - establish relations — forecast/time + demand
obj - predict something

multiple regression → when have more than one determinant
— establish how income relates to consumption

income consumption
I → C
input output
independent dependent

aging = f(time)   dep

% of Defects
# of inspections
indep

Chapter VIII

REGRESSION AND CORRELATION ANALYSIS

(handwritten right margin) directly + pos. relat

Often it becomes desirable to define a particular relationship
between variables. For example, a new instrument based on nuclear
principles is available for testing density. Not only is it relatively
speedy, it also avoids the need for cutting and weighing as called for
by conventional methods. Before the new instrument is accepted, however, we must know with some precision just how well it performs and
how the measurements obtained with it relate to -- or, in other words,
correlate with -- the conventional method. Usually a line of average
relationship, known as the "regression line" defines the correspond-
ences between the two variables, such as density by nuclear versus conventional method. Next, a correlation coefficient gives an indication
how good the agreement between the two variables is.

(handwritten right margin) linear — st. line

As a further illustration, we may be interested in evaluating the
effect of increased helix angle of a twisted strand on its elongation
characteristics. Again, a line or curve of relationship and its correlation coefficient are needed, if we are to predict the optimum helix
angle for a desired strand elongation. Finally, in production it may
become necessary to evaluate the relation of increased processing
speeds, humidities, temperatures, pressures or other variables on the
quality, productivity and yield of output.

(handwritten right margin) inversely related neg

The types of relationships described abound. We can approximate
most of them from experience. But management decisions can be made
more efficiently if the relationships between important variables can
be defined in relatively precise terms. The regression line and correlation analysis permit us to attain this objective.

Input and Output Variables

A job shop had noted a large degree of fluctuation in the variety
of items processed from week to week. Preliminary study of accounting
data showed that cost per item seemed to increase with increased number of different items produced in any week. In order to establish a
more precise relationship between the two variables, a correlation
study was recommended.

The cost per item is thus viewed as a function of variety of items
per week. Cost is the output or response which depends upon the input
of variety of items processed. We may also say that variety is the independent variable, receiving the symbol X; while the dependent variable Y, is the cost. In many instances of course, such an analysis may
show that a cause-and-effect system which may have been expected does,
in truth, not exist.

The distinction between input and output variables comes from log-
ic, common sense and engineering judgment. As an extreme example, it
would certainly be nonsense to claim that time is a function of aging
or that compression is caused by density of the material produced.

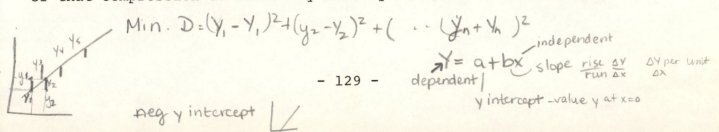

(handwritten)
$$\text{Min. } D = (y_1 - Y_1)^2 + (y_2 - Y_2)^2 + (\cdots (y_n + Y_n)^2$$

$Y = a + bx$ slope   rise/run $\frac{\Delta Y}{\Delta x}$ ΔY per unit Δx

dependent
independent

y intercept — value y at x=0

neg y intercept

- 129 -

Time makes for aging and compression for density, not vice versa. But the distinctions are not always that clear. For example, in comparing the test results of a new versus an older principle of measurement of friction, strength, thickness, density or moisture, which of the two is dependent and which is the independent variable? We may find it convenient to call the new instrument "independent" and evaluate the closeness with which it obtains the values of the old instrument as the "dependent" variable. But the distinction is arbitrary, and many would reverse the definitions, calling the old instrument independent and the new one dependent.

ASSIGNMENT VIII-1:

The following will serve to develop a sense of distinction between dependent and independent variables.

1. It was desired to evaluate the effect of number of people at work assembling high precision micro-miniaturized items in a nearly dust-free white room. The white room population varied and so did the contamination level in terms of dust particles. Which variable is dependent, Y, and which independent, X. (circle one).

    a. White Room Population: <u>X</u> or <u>Y</u>

    b. Contaminant Level: <u>X</u> or <u>Y</u>

2. Many football experts claim that ball control is important. You have decided to check this statement against recent data on various teams, their "first downs" (a measure of ball control) and their scores. Indicate:

    a. Independent variable, X:_____

    b. Dependent variable, Y:_____

3. A large group of similar plants is comparing the results of efforts to insure greater safety in operations. For each plant there is available (a) the annual hours of lost-time accidents and (b) the expenditures on safety, such as safety-committee meetings, posters, guard rail programs, elimination of hazardous conditions and related activity. Indicate:

    a. Independent variable:_____

    b. Dependent variable:_____

4. A laundry has observed that with age the pressboard covers tend to harden, resulting in an increased incidence of broken buttons while press-ironing shirts*. Indicate:

---

*Example adapted from the Case "Spotless Laundry" in Enrick, N.L. Cases in Management Statistics, 1962, Holt Rinehart & Winston Inc., New York, N.Y. 10017.

a. Independent variable:_____

b. Dependent variable:_____

5. A ductile iron foundry has observed a certain predictability of compressive strength of castings based on simple hardness determinations. Indicate:

a. Independent variable:_____

b. Dependent variable:_____

ASSIGNMENT VIII-2:

Based on the illustrations above, review your own experience (business, industrial or other field) to give three examples of variables for which a relationship has been found or may reasonably be expected to exist:

Subject Matter	Independent Variable	Dependent Variable
1._____	_____	_____
2._____	_____	_____
3._____	_____	_____

Illustrative Example

The Production and Engineering Departments of a company had embarked on a program of setting more realistic population standards and parts tolerances. On one of the machines, it was found that a variety of different cutting speeds had been used on similar components. Moreover, the product tolerances attained with each speed could be compiled readily from the inspection records. (The term "tolerances attained" represents process capability or "process spread" at each speed, not the tolerance that might be specified later, based on a knowledge of process capability.)

The data appear in Table VIII-1, columns for cutting speed, X, and process spread, Y. For example, a cutting speed of 42 feet per minute (fpm) yielded a process spread of 85 in 0.001 inch and a speed of 45 gave a tolerance of 83 in 0.001 inch. (For the time being, examine only these two columns.)

Plotting the Data

Graphing of the two variables, each containing 5 values, leads to a scatter diagram of 5 points as in Figure VIII-1. For X = 42 and Y = 85, for example, we enter the base or X-axis of the diagram at the scale mark 42 and proceed vertically upward to the level 85, corresponding to the Y-axis or ordinate. The intersection, shown by means of a small circle, presents the relation of X and Y for this one point. All 5 points are obtained in this manner.

Table VIII-1. RELATION OF CUTTING SPEED TO PROCESS SPREAD

(Small Letters x and y show Cutting Speed X and Process Spread Y as Deviations from Their Respective Averages)

[handwritten: original] [handwritten: deviation form]

Part No.	Speed X	Spread Y	Deviations x	Deviations y	Squares x^2	Squares y^2	Cross Product xy
1	42	85	-9*	-4	81	16	36
2	45	83	-6	-6	36	36	36
3	52	90	1	1	1	1	1
4	56	92	5	3	25	9	15
5	60	95	9	6	81	36	54
Totals:	255	445	0	0	224	98	142
Means	51	89					

[handwritten: $Y = a + bx$, spread speed]

Regression Line, $Y_c = a + bK$:

$$b = \Sigma xy / \Sigma x^2 = 142/224 = 0.63 = \text{Slope}$$

[handwritten: avg of raw data]

$$a = \overline{Y} - b\overline{X} = 89 - (0.63)51 = 56.87 = \underline{Y}\text{-Intercept}$$

$$Y_c = 56.87 + 0.63X$$

[handwritten: $56.87 - 0.63X$ would be neg. related]

For example, for X = 40, $Y_c = 56.87 + 0.63(40) = 82.07$

Error Standard Deviation (also known as Standard Error of Estimate):

[handwritten: Variance]

$$\sigma^2_{error} = \sigma_e^2 = (\Sigma y^2 - b\Sigma yx)/(n-2) = (98 - 0.63 \times 142)/(5-2)$$

[handwritten: $SD = \sqrt{\sigma^2} = \sigma$]

$$= 2.85$$

$$\sigma_e = \sqrt{2.85} = 1.68$$

[handwritten: n-2 parameters, 2pts to establish line]

Correlation Coefficient:

$$r^2 = \text{Coefficient of Determination} = b\Sigma xy / \Sigma y^2 = (0.63)142/98 = 0.91$$

[handwritten: % of variance explained due to variable (variance of y explained by X)]

$$r = \text{Correlation Coefficient} = \sqrt{0.91} = 0.955$$

[handwritten: Measure of direction & relationship] [handwritten: (highly correlated) + positively correlated]

Confidence Limits Around Regression Line

At 95% Level, or $\pm 2\sigma_e = \pm 2(1.68) = \pm 3.36$

at 99.7% Level or $\pm 3\sigma_e = \pm 3(1.68) = \pm 5.04$

---

*For example, 42 - 51 = -9 in terms of deviations of X from $\overline{X}$.

[handwritten: high correlation] [handwritten: lower correl]

[handwritten: correlation close to zero variables indep of each other]

[handwritten: correlation → doesn't mean cause & effect]

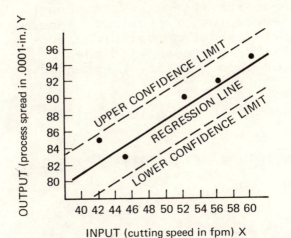

Figure VIII-1. Scatter diagram. Relation of input and output variables, the regression line and confidence limits are shown. The 5 points come from the basic data, the regression line has been computed to show the average relationship among the 5 points. The confidence limits are comparable to control limits on a control chart.

ASSIGNMENT VIII-3:

In order to test your skill at entering points on a scatter diagram, assume that there had been a 6th part for which we had found a process spread of 94 with a cutting speed of 48. Indicate this point in light pencil in Figure VIII-1.

1. Does the plotted point fall in line with the general trend of the prior five points? (yes/no).

_____

2. If the answer is "no", what reason might there be for this out-of-control point?_____

_____

3. What do you conclude if the plotted point does fall in line?

_____

_____

_____

Regression Line

The Regression Line reveals the average relationship between two variables, X and Y. For each computed value of Y, indicated by the symbol Y_c and pronounced "Y-computed," the equation of the Line (From Table VIII-1, row n) is found to be:

$$Y_c = 56.9 + 0.63X$$

Accordingly, if X is, say, 40, we multiply it by the coefficient 0.63. Thus, 40 x 0.63 = 25.2. Adding this 25.2 to the constant of 56.9 gives the value of 82.1 for Y_c corresponding to X = 40. Next, for X = 60, Y_c becomes 94.7 by similar calculations; viz., 60 x 0.63 added to the constant 56.9 as given by the equation above.

Now, connect these two points thereby obtaining the regression line.

We may observe in passing that the X and Y axes of the graph happen to intersect at X = 38 and Y = 78. Had we chosen to set them at zero for each axis and had we then extended the regression line downward to the right, it would have intercepted the Y-axis at the point 56.9, known as the "Y-intercept". In all regression lines, the constant of the equations represents the level at which it crosses the Y-axis, provided the X and Y axes have been drawn to intersect at X = Y = 0. This cross-over point thus represents the geometric meaning of the constant in the regression equation. The coefficient of X, in the equation, indicates the slope of the line or its steepness. Although our example showed an ascending line, a descending or negative slope is often encountered. For example, the relation of number of defects remaining in a production lot will (hopefully) decrease with the amount of inspection effort (independent or input variable) expended.

ASSIGNMENT VIII-4:

Assume that the regression equation had been as follows:

$$Y_c = 40 + 0.8X$$

Now compute values of Y_c for various values of X, utilizing the space below:

(a) Assumed Value of X	(b) Calculated Value of 0.8 x X	(c) Y Intercept	Result, Y_c = b + c
40	_____	_____	_____
50	_____	_____	_____
60	_____	_____	_____

Value of Regression Line

In place of the calculated regression line, we could also do relatively well by drawing in a free-hand approximation. There are, however, some reasons why this may not be desirable:

1. When the relationship is not very distinct and points are relatively scattered, it becomes difficult to draw a free-hand line that does justice to every point.

2. In any event, free-hand lines will differ from person to person. A computed line will remain the same (barring errors in arithmetic and geometry of drawing).

3. Today, the task of drawing lines -- particularly when the points are many -- is relegated to the computer. That equipment is incapable of such a task unless there is an equation from which to work.

The regression line is also known as the "least squares line" because it minimizes the square of the vertical distances of each point with regard to the line. No other straight line can accomplish this objective.

Standard Error of Estimate

The Standard Error of Estimate is really a Standard Deviation, based on the average of the squared deviations of the plotted points with respect to the regression line. In particular, we measure and square the vertical distance of each point from the computed line, sum the squares, divide by the number of tests, and take the square root. The familiar factors of 2.0 and 3.0 from the Normal Curve then yield the well-known 95 and 99.7 percent confidence limits respectively. The interpretation of these limits is similar to control limits. For 95 percent limits, we may expect that in practice only 1 point out of 20 will fall outside either limit as a result of chance fluctuations. For 99.7 percent the corresponding ratio is 3 out of 1000.

The calculations will be self-explanatory from the illustration in Table VIII-1. Note that the Standard Error of Estimate is also known as the "Standard Deviation around Regression Line," which is more direct designation.

ASSIGNMENT VIII-5:

Assume that the Standard Error of Estimate had been 1.5, and compute:

1. Upper Confidence Limit, at 95%: _____ inch.

2. Lower Confidence Limi6, at 95%: _____

3. Upper 99.7% Confidence Limit: _____

4. Lower 99.7% Confidence Limit: _____

Interpretation of Correlation Coefficient

The larger the absolute numerical value of the correlation coefficient, the stronger the relationship between the variables investigated. If in Figure VIII-1 all points had fallen in one line, we would have considered the correlation at $r = 1.0$ as perfect. Yet, the data would have been suspect. Rarely would we expect in the laboratory or in the plant a perfect relationship. Errors of measurements, chance fluctuations and other factors will usually contribute some variability. The sliding scale in Table VIII-2 is based on predominant opinions, but interpretations vary with individuals and with the type of problem investigated.

When a relatively small number of points have been correlated, it is possible that a high value of r may have been obtained because of chance fluctuations of sampling, testing and processing. In order to rule out chance, we must make a statistical significance test, using the critical values of Table VIII-3. For the illustrative example of speeds and tolerances, the correlation was "excellent," and there is also significance at the 95 percent level or better. We have thus a relatively high degree of assurance that, despite only 5 data points, and thus only 5 - 2 = 3 Degrees of Freedom, our findings are valid.

ASSIGNMENT VIII-6: Review Problem

Four volunteers were subjected to simulated conditions of stress as might occur under certain space travel emergencies. Upon a signal by each volunteer, tests were terminated. Next the loss in reaction

Table VIII-2. Values for Interpretation of Correlation Coefficients

Coefficient of Correlation, r, Observed	General Interpretation of the Relationship Observed
1.0	Perfect
0.9	Excellent
0.8	Very Good
0.7	Good
0.6	Fair
0.5	Borderline
0.4	Poor
0.3	Negligible
to	to
0.0	Nonexistent

Notes:

1. A correlation coefficient can never be higher than 1.0.

2. The interpretation of the correlation coefficient is not affected by the fact that a minus sign may precede it. The sign merely indicates the slope of the regression line. An r of -0.9 represents "excellent correlation" with a negative slope of the regression line. (Such a line would run downward, from left-to-right on the scatter diagram, as against an upward line for positive sign.)

3. A correlation coefficient can never be less than -1.0.

4. Even though a correlation coefficient is considered "poor" or negligible, it may nevertheless be "significant," in the sense that the relationship observed can be demonstrated at some confidence level as not being purely "chance." But significant correlation, by itself, is not very meaningful. Thus a coefficient of correlation of 0.4 at 95 percent significance means: "The relationship observed is very poor, but we can state at 95 percent confidence (5 percent risk of error) that the relationship is not a chance coincidence of data-points." Conversely, if a high value of r is associated with "no significance," it means that an inadequate number of data-points are available to demonstrate significance of what may otherwise be a perfect or excellent correlation.

Table VIII-3. Minimum Values of The Correlation Coefficient Needed
To Establish Statistical Significance

Degrees of Freedom[a]	Significance Evaluation[b]	
	90 Percent Confidence Level	95 Percent Confidence Level
2	0.90	0.95
3	0.81	0.88
4	0.73	0.81
5	0.67	0.75
6	0.62	0.71
8	0.55	0.63
10	0.50	0.58
15	0.41	0.48
20	0.36	0.42
25	0.32	0.38
30	0.30	0.35
40	0.26	0.30
50	0.23	0.27
60	0.21	0.25
80	0.18	0.22
100	0.16	0.20

[a]Degrees of Freedom, in correlation analysis, refers to the number of data-points in the scatter-diagram less 2, or in other words N - 2. Note that any two points can always be connected by a straight line, or in other words the first two points alone would not give a valid estimate of correlation at any time. Hence the use of N - 2 for Degrees of Freedom.

[b]The use of the table is best shown by an example. Assume that N = 5 and the correlation coefficient, r, found is 0.96. Degrees of Freedom, D F = N - 2 = 5 - 2 = 3. Referring to the line for D F of 3, we observe that the smallest coefficient needed for the 95 percent significance is 0.88. The actual value of r exceeded this 0.88, and is therefore significant. A value of r of 0.81 would have been significant at 90 percent. A value of r of 0.7 would have been not significant (chance could have produced it with only 3 D F), even though the coefficient of correlation as such is a good one. The suggestion, then, is that with more testing we may be able to establish significance.

Source: "Percentage points for the distribution of the correlation co-efficient," with adaptations from Biometrika Tables for Statis-ticians, Vol. I, edited by E.S. Pearson and H.O. Hartley, Cambridge University Press, 1958.

time (as a decimal fraction of a second) was related to stress time in hours:

Volun-teer	Stress Hrs., X	Loss, Y	x	y	x^2	y^2	xy
A	5	0.10	-4	-.20			
B	8	0.40	-1	+.10			
C	10	0.30	1	0			
D	13	0.40	4	+.10			
	36	1.20	0	0			
Means	9	0.30					

FIND:

1. Regression Line, $Y_c = a + bX$

   Slope b = ___$\Sigma xy / \Sigma x^2$___ = _____ .

   Y-Intercept, a = ___$\overline{Y} - b\overline{X}$___ = _____ .

   Y_c = ___$Y-I$___ + ___$slope$___ X.

2. Error Standard Deviation,

   σ_e^2 = ___$\Sigma y^2 - b\Sigma xy / n-2$___ σ_e^2 = _____ .

   Correlation Coefficient,

   r^2 = ___$b\Sigma xy / \Sigma y^2$___   r = _____ .

3. 95% Confidence Limits around Regression Line: ± ___$2\sigma_e$___ .

ANSWER THESE QUESTIONS:

1. What is the general interpretation of the relationship observed? _____
   _____ .

2. Using the scale for quality of the correlation coefficient (from "perfect" to "nonexistent"), indicate the quality for r above: _____ .

3. Is the correlation significant? yes/no _____ .

4. Assuming a volunteer is stressed for 15 hours, what is the expected loss in reaction time, based on the relation found above? _____ seconds.

5. Why is it dangerous to make extrapolations, such as for Question 4? _____
   _____
   _____ .

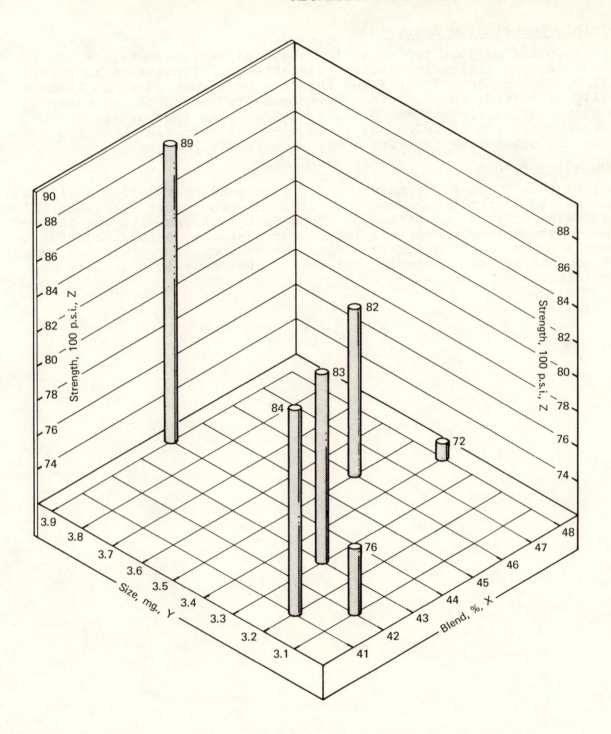

Figure VIII-2. Three-dimensional correlation diagram. The effect of blending percentage X, and particle size Y jointly on burst strength Z is plotted. A relationship is apparent from this presentation, from high strength at higher size values and lower blending percentages to low strength at lower sizes and higher blending percentages.

Multiple Correlation Analysis

In place of just two variables, several variables may be involved. A correlation involving 3 variables is illustrated in Figure VIII-2. The number of variables that can be investigated is theoretically unlimited, and computers have been programmed to correlate up to 50 variables. Problems do arise, however, in that an assumption of relatively linear relations is made -- while in fact U-shaped relations and other non-linearities may be markedly present.

Concluding Points

In this Chapter, we have briefly discussed correlation analysis. Because the arithmetic becomes complex, only one minor assignment plus one review problem are included. This is in keeping with the primary need to understand the principles of correlation. Actual computations today are done electronically. With the subject of correlation, also, the general topic of experimental design and analysis will have been completed.

GLOSSARY OF STATISTICAL TERMS

It is apparent that many of the terms used in industrial experimentation have special meanings which can be best understood "operationally" -- by showing how they work under specific conditions. Therefore, this glossary should only supplement the operational examples given throughout the book. To obtain an exact understanding of each term, the preceding text should be carefully reviewed.

Average. A measure of central tendency of a set of data. The most frequently used average is the arithmetic mean, $\overline{X}$, obtained by totaling the individual values and dividing the total by the number, n, of units used. Thus, $\overline{X} = \Sigma X/n$.

Balance. The various factors and conditions of an experiment must be balanced in order to give each an equal opportunity to show how it affects the response. Without balancing, some factors may receive improper weights to influence the response and the subsequent evaluation of the experiment. Failure to balance may also result in undesired confounding of factors and their effects.

Chance. The random element in experimentation, sampling, testing, materials and processes which is caused by a large number of continuously operating but very minute factors. Statistical methodology permits us to distinguish between that range of small fluctuations assignable to a system of chance causes, or "luck of the draw" as compared to real factors (mistakes, shifting of settings, faulty operation) that need correction. See also ERROR.

Confidence Interval. The magnitude of difference between two arithmetical averages of a group, which may be expected as a result of chance experimental-error fluctuations at a specific confidence level.

Confidence Level. The relative assurance, in percent, that a specific observation is not caused by chance experimental-error fluctuations. For example, a 95% confidence level indicates that we are 95% "sure" that an observed difference between two averages or other observations is representative of a "real" -- not a "chance" -- effect.

Confidence Limit. The limit, usually measured in terms of ± deviations from the average (or line of average relationship, or other central value), within which a certain percentage of the true values of a population may be expected to fall, at a given confidence level. Thus, 99.7 percent of all population values may be expected to fall within an area given by a regression line ±3 standard errors (of estimate).

Confounding. The arrangement of experimental factors in such a way that the effect of some of them cannot be separately distinguished. Confounding may occur as a result of faulty design of experiments. However, it can be deliberate, in which case the experimenter knows that his design will result in some confounding, but time factors or other limitations do not permit a design that is completely free of confounding.

Control. A state in which observed variations remain within limits expected by chance at a given confidence level. See also CHANCE.

Control Limit. The limit within which an observed set of variations may be considered to exhibit chance fluctuations. Control Limits are usually established at a desired confidence level (such as 90, 95, or 99.7 percent) or risk (such as 10, 5 or 0.3 percent).

Correlation Coefficient. A measure of the association between the values of two (or more) variables. The degree of this relationship is expressed in terms of a scale, with 1.0 representing perfect correlation and 0 representing no correlation. When two variables, x and y, are involved, the correlation coefficient is said to be positive if high values of x are associated with high values of y; negative if high values of x are associated with low values of y. A + or - sign merely indicates the direction, not the magnitude of correlation. Therefore, a correlation of -0.9 is not of lesser importance than one of +0.9.

Degrees of Freedom. A term applicable in the evaluation of variance. In the most simple cases, when the variance is estimated from a relatively small number (n) of tests or replications (r), the degrees of freedom (D F) is n - 1 or r - 1. In complex experiments, which may seek variances from several factors, further adjustments in the degrees-of-freedom formula are required.

Determination. The testing, measurement or other determination, appraisal or observation of a sample unit or experimental unit. Sometimes, several determinations are made on one unit before a single test result is recorded. When several determinations are made per unit, it is usually the average that is recorded. Note that the average of n determinations becomes just one sample or experimental unit.

Error. Sampling error and testing error are considered unavoidable aspects of sampling testing and experimentation even under the most favorable conditions. Only when the small range of fluctuations allowable as "error" is exceeded can we speak of a findable mistake. Error is to be expected, mistakes are to be avoided.

See also CHANCE.

Experimental Error. Fluctuations in experimental data which are caused by unavoidable chance fluctuations in testing, sampling, materials, equipment, human and environmental factors, despite proper skill, care and circumspection.

Factor Levels. The points of a factor which are studied by the experiment. For example, an experiment designed to study the effect on scrap of three machine speeds, 50, 55, and 60 rpm, using four different materials, A, B, C and D, has the following:

- Factor of machine speeds at 3 levels: 50, 55 and 60 rpm.

- Factor of materials at 4 levels: A, B, C and D.

Note that one group of factor levels is defined quantitatively (in terms of speed), while the other factor levels can only be defined by "name" designations. Levels may also be expressed qualitatively in such terms as "tight" or "loose," "sharp" or "blunt," etc.

F-Ratio. The ratio of two meansquares. The F-ratio is used to ascertain whether or not the main effect of a factor or the interaction effect of two or more factors is significant at a desired confidence level.

Interaction. The influence of one factor on the effect of another factor. Interaction is zero if the effect of either factor is the same at all levels of the remaining factor.

Meansquare. A statistical term used in the analysis of variance. The ratio of factor and interaction meansquares to the experimental error meansquare is the F-ratio, which is used to evaluate significance. From the meansquare, the variance components of an experiment may be determined.

Normal Curve. The particular pattern of a bell-shaped frequency distribution, formed from a set of data. It represents the most commonly expected form of chance occurrences. Other distributions occur and can be dealt with by appropriate statistical procedures.

Out-of-Control. A data-point that falls outside the limits expected by chance at a given confidence level. Operating within the management-by-exception principle, an out-of-control occurrence calls for managerial attention (and correction).

$\overline{R}$ (R-bar). Average of sum of individual ranges used to compute control limits for variables control charts.

Randomization. A plan to avoid the conscious or unconscious bias which may arise from an orderly selection of samples for an experiment.

Range (R). Difference between the highest and lowest reading in a set of data, it represents the most commonly expected form of chance occurrences. Other distributions occur and can be dealt with by appropriate statistical procedures.

Regression. A relationship between two or more variables with these characteristics: One or more of the variables is subject to random or chance fluctuations known as "sampling and testing error " (where "error" does not refer to a mistake, but rather to unavoidable fluctuations); and the average relationship among the variables can be shown by an equation.

Regresssion Line. A line showing the average relationship between two variables, one being an input or independent variable, and the other being an output or dependent variable. One characteristic of this line of average relationship is that the squared deviations of the actual points (of the scatter diagram), measured in terms of vertical distances to the regression line', will be at a minimum. Therefore, the line is also known as a "least-squares" line.

GLOSSARY OF STATISTICAL TERMS

Replication. The use of repeat trials in experimentation. For example, if machine speeds are tested at 3 factor levels of 50, 55 and 60 rpm and each speed is run twice, the number of replications (r) is 2. If each speed is run three times, r = 3, etc.

Response. The test results obtained from an experiment. Response may occur in several forms, such as quality, efficiency, reliability or cost. For example, response in terms of "yield percent" is a measure of efficiency; "scrap percent" is a measure of quality; and "mean-time-between-failures" is a measure of reliability. In some experiments, responses may occur in more than one form.

Risk. The likelihood, as a fraction or percent, that a sample may give an erroneous indication of lot quality. See also CONFIDENCE LEVEL.

σ (Greek Symbol). Pronounced "sigma," this small Greek letter indicates the " tandard Deviation," a statistical measure of variability. See also STANDARD DEVIATION.

Σ (Greek Symbol). Pronounced "sum of," this large Greek Sigma indicates that a total follows.

Sample. A collection of specimens or sample units. The sample size represents the number of specimens or number of sample units. The use of "sample" to indicate a "specimen" is improper, excepting in those rare instances where an entire sample consists of only one single sample unit. In experimentation, an experimental unit is equivalent to a sample unit. See also DETERMINATION.

Sample Size. The number of sample units comprising a sample. A sample may consist of only one sample unit, but usually there are at least two sample units.

Significance. The condition wherein an observation can be considered to be non-chance at a particular stated confidence level. This statistical designation of significance is in purely probabilistic terms, and is not related to technological significance or economic importance. However any observation not supported by statistical significance may be erroneous (sampling error, chance flunctuations, etc.).

Standard Deviation (σ). A measure of variability. It represents the square root of the average of the squared deviations of individual values from their own group average. Denoting the individual values X and the averages $\overline{X}$, the Standard Deviation, is represented by:

$$\sigma^2 = \frac{\Sigma(X - \overline{X})^2}{n-1} = \frac{\Sigma X^2 - (\Sigma X)^2/n}{n-1}$$

Standard Error of the Mean, $\sigma_{\overline{X}}$. When experimental error is measured in terms of its estimated standard deviation (s), the standard error is obtained from $s/\sqrt{n}$, where (n) is the sample size. Note that $\sigma_{\overline{X}}$ is often referred to briefly as "Standard Error."

Standard Error of Estimate. A measure of variability of individual plotted points of a scatter diagram to the Line of Average Relationship or Regression estimated for the variables whose correlation is being studied.

Variable. A magnitude that can vary. For example, tensile strength in pounds, degrees temperature of a solution, fineness in micrograms, or thickness in 100ths inch.

Variance (σ^2). The square of the Standard Deviation. See also STANDARD DEVIATION. Because variation exhibits properties requiring vectorial addition of components, the Standard Deviation is not linearly additive, while the variance is.

Variance Component. In an experiment involving many factors, interactions and an error term, separate variances representing each factor, each interaction, and the error can be calculated. The addition of these individual variance components yields the total variance. "Variance" and "variance component" are often used interchangeably.

Variation Coefficient (V). A measure of relative variation, in percent obtained from the ratio of Standard Deviation to Arithmetic Mean of a set of data.

$\overline{X}$ (X-bar). See Average.

$\overline{\overline{X}}$ (X double bar): Grand average of a sum of averages, $\overline{X}$'s, or of the sum of individual observations from which such averages were computed.

$\overline{X}$ - R Chart. Control Chart using average, $\overline{X}$, and Range, R, control charts in combination to define normal operating units and variation for a process or operation.

APPENDIX

based on 95% CI

Table 1. Factors q for Confidence Interval Estimation

Degrees of Freedom	Number k of Averages in a Set													
	2	3	4	5	6	7	8	9	10	12	14	16	18	20
1	18	27	33	37	40	43	45	47	49	52	54	56	58	60
2	6.1	8.3	9.8	11	12	12	13	13	14	15	16	16	16	17
3	4.6	5.9	6.8	7.5	8.0	8.5	8.8	9.2	9.5	10	10	11	11	11
4	3.9	5.0	5.8	6.3	6.7	7.0	7.4	7.6	7.8	8.2	8.5	8.0	9.0	9.2
5	3.6	4.6	5.2	5.7	6.0	6.3	6.6	6.8	7.0	7.3	7.6	7.8	8.0	8.2
6	3.5	4.3	4.9	5.3	5.6	5.9	6.1	6.3	6.5	6.8	7.0	7.2	7.4	7.6
7	3.3	4.2	4.7	5.1	5.4	5.6	5.8	6.0	6.2	6.4	6.7	6.8	7.0	7.2
8	3.3	4.0	4.4	4.8	5.2	5.4	5.6	5.8	5.9	6.2	6.4	6.6	6.7	6.9
9	3.2	4.0	4.4	4.8	5.0	5.2	5.4	5.6	5.7	5.9	6.2	6.4	6.5	6.6
10	3.2	3.9	4.4	4.6	4.9	5.1	5.3	5.5	5.6	5.8	5.8	6.2	6.3	6.5
12	3.1	3.8	4.2	4.5	4.8	5.0	5.1	5.3	5.4	5.6	5.8	6.0	6.1	6.2
15	3.0	3.7	4.1	4.4	4.6	4.8	4.9	5.1	5.2	5.4	5.6	5.7	5.8	6.0
20	3.0	3.6	4.0	4.2	4.4	4.6	4.8	4.9	5.0	5.2	5.4	5.5	5.6	5.7
30	2.9	3.5	3.8	4.1	4.3	4.5	4.6	4.7	4.8	5.0	5.2	5.3	5.4	5.5
60	2.8	3.4	3.7	4.0	4.2	4.3	4.4	4.5	4.6	4.8	4.9	5.1	5.2	5.2
120	2.8	3.4	3.4	3.9	4.1	4.2	4.4	4.5	4.6	4.7	4.8	5.0	5.1	5.1

<u>Notes</u> 1. Degrees of Freedom, D F shown is associated with the experimental-error estimate represented by the Standard Deviation, σ.

2. Confidence Intervals, CI at the 95 Percent Confidence (and thus 5 Percent Sampling Risk Level) are obtained from:

$$CI = q \times \sigma / \sqrt{n}$$

where q is tabulated, as above, and n is the sample size on which each experimental average is based.

<u>Example</u>: Given a σ of 2.7, with D F =4, and k =2 Averages to be compared, each Average based on a sample size n =4, then q from D F - row 4 an k-column 2 is found to be 3.9. Next,

$$CI = 3.9 \times 2.7 / \sqrt{4} = 5.3$$

The observed difference between the two Averages must be equal to or greater than 5.3 in order to be considered significant at the 95 percent confidence level.

Source:"Upper 5-Percent Points of the Studentized Range" by E.S. Pearson and H.O. Hartley, in <u>Biometrika Tables</u>, p. 176, Cambridge University Press (1956).

Table 2. Conversion Factors, F_d, for Estimated Standard
Deviation From Average Range of Sampling Data

Sample Size or Replications, n	Conversion Factor, F_d	
	Exact	Rounded
2	0.886	0.9
3	0.591	0.6
4	0.486	0.5
5	0.430	0.43
6	0.395	0.40
7	0.370	0.37
8	0.351	0.35
9	0.337	0.34
10	0.325	0.32
12	0.307	0.31

Notes:

1. The use of Average Range, $\overline{R}$, is less precise than the estimation of true standard deviation by means of the more laborious sums-of-squared deviations calculations.

2. Example

    Given an Average Range, $\overline{R}$ of 3.0, based on sample size r = 2 for each R, then the Factor F_d = 0.9 (using the rounded method), giving for the Standard Deviation 3.0 x 0.9 = 2.7.

Source: Factors F_d are the reciprocals of factors d_2 given by L.H.C. Tippett, "On the Extreme Individuals and the Range of Samples Taken from Normal Population", Biometrika (1925) 17:364-387.

(handwritten note: if greater than 25 n instead of n-1)

Table 3. Critical Values of The F-Ratio for Significance Testing

(5 Percent Risk or 95 Percent Confidence Level)

Denominator Degrees of Freedom*	Numerator Degrees Freedom*											
	1	2	3	4	5	6	8	10	15	30	60	1
1	161	200	216	225	230	234	239	242	246	250	252	25
2	18.5	19.0	19.2	19.2	19.3	19.3	19.4	19.4	19.4	19.5	19.5	19.
3	10.1	9.6	9.3	9.1	9.0	8.9	8.8	8.8	8.7	8.6	8.6	8.
4	7.7	6.9	6.6	6.4	6.3	6.2	6.0	6.0	5.9	5.7	5.7	5.
5	6.6	5.8	5.4	5.2	5.1	5.0	4.8	4.7	4.6	4.5	4.4	4.
6	6.0	5.1	4.8	4.5	4.4	4.3	4.1	4.1	4.0	3.8	3.7	3.
7	5.6	4.7	4.3	4.1	4.0	3.9	3.7	3.6	3.5	3.4	3.3	3.
8	5.3	4.5	4.1	3.8	3.7	3.6	3.4	3.3	3.2	3.1	3.0	3.
10	5.0	4.1	3.7	3.5	3.3	3.2	3.1	3.0	2.8	2.7	2.6	2.
12	4.7	3.9	3.5	3.3	3.1	3.0	2.8	2.8	2.6	2.5	2.4	2.
15	4.5	3.7	3.3	3.1	3.0	2.8	2.6	2.5	2.4	2.2	2.2	2.
20	4.4	3.5	3.1	2.9	2.7	2.6	2.4	2.3	2.2	2.0	1.9	1.
25	4.2	3.4	3.0	2.8	2.6	2.5	2.3	2.2	2.1	1.9	1.8	1.
30	4.2	3.3	2.9	2.7	2.5	2.4	2.3	2.2	2.0	1.8	1.7	1.
40	4.1	3.2	2.8	2.6	2.5	2.3	2.2	2.1	1.9	1.7	1.6	1.
60	4.0	3.2	2.8	2.5	2.4	2.3	2.0	1.9	1.8	1.6	1.5	1.
120	3.9	3.1	2.7	2.4	2.3	2.2	2.0	1.8	1.7	1.5	1.4	1.

Example 1:

Given MS Between = 32, with DF = 1, and MS Error = 3, with DF = 7. Then the observed F-ratio is 32/3 = 10.7. The tabulated critical value for Numerator DF = 3 and Denominator DF = 7 is 4.3. Since the observed F (10.7) is greater than the tabulated minimum F needed for significance (4.3), the observed differences among the means are considered significant at the 95 percent level of confidence. The tabulated F is also called the critical F.

Example 2:

Given MS Between = 8, with DF = 2, and MS Error = 2, with DF = 5. Then the observed F = 8/2 = 4, the critical F is 5.8, and the differences among the means are not significant at the 95 percent level.

---

*   The Degrees of Freedom, DF, associated with the numerator and denominator of the F-ratio jointly determine the tabular, critical value of F. Only if the observed F equals or exceeds the critical value is the difference among means significant.

Table 4. Critical Rank Values For EVOP Analysis

Number of Cycles	Two Input Variables[a]		Three Input Variables[b]	
	95% Level	99% Level	95% Level	99% Level
3	3	↓	3	↓
4	5	4	6	5
5	7	5	9	7
6	9	7	12	10
7	12	9	16	13
8	16	12	20	16

Notes:

↓ Arrows indicate that more cycles will be needed for significance determination at the stated confidence level of 99 percent. In any case, at least 3 cycles are needed.

a Two input variables represents 2 Factors each at 2 levels plus 1 center point, or $2^2 + 1 = 5$ treatment combinations.

b Three input variables represents 3 Factors each at 2 levels plus 1 center point, or $2^3 + 1 = 9$ treatment combinations.

Interpretation:

In EVOP, if the actual lowest rank sum after a given number of cycles is equal to or less than the Critical Rank Value listed above, significance at the indicated confidence level (95 or 99 percent) has been demonstrated. No assumptions regarding the nature of the distribution (normal or not) need be made with this significance test method.

Source: Computed by N.L. Enrick for all 99 Percent Levels and for phases 6 to 8 of the 95 Percent Levels. The concept of critical rank sums and the remaining values of the table are due to Dr. Marvin Zelen.

Table 5. A Table of Random Numbers

Line	(1)	(2)	(3)	(4)	(5)	(6)	(7)	(8)
1	78994	36244	02673	25475	84953	61793	50243	63423
2	04909	58485	70686	93930	34880	73059	06823	80257
3	46582	73570	33004	51795	86477	46736	60460	70345
4	29242	89792	88634	60285	07190	07795	27011	85941
5	68104	81339	97090	20601	78940	20228	22802	96070
6	17156	02182	82504	19880	93747	80910	78260	25136
7	50711	94789	07171	02103	99057	98775	37997	18325
8	39449	52409	75095	77720	39729	03205	09313	43545
9	75629	82729	76916	72657	58992	32756	01154	84890
10	01020	55151	36132	51971	32155	60735	64867	35424
11	08337	89989	24260	08618	66798	25889	52860	57375
12	76829	47229	19706	30094	68430	92399	98749	22081
13	39708	30641	21267	56501	95182	72442	21445	17276
14	89836	55817	56747	75195	06818	83043	47403	58266
15	25903	61370	66081	54076	67442	52964	23823	02718
16	71345	03422	01015	68025	19703	77313	04555	83425
17	61454	92263	14647	08473	34124	10740	40839	05620
18	80376	08909	30470	40200	46558	61742	11643	92121
19	45144	54373	05505	90074	24783	86299	20900	15144
20	12191	88527	58852	51175	11534	87218	04876	85584
21	62936	59120	73957	35969	21598	47287	39394	08778
22	31588	96798	43668	12611	01714	77266	55079	24690
23	20787	96048	84726	17512	39450	43618	30629	24356
24	45603	00745	84635	43079	52724	14262	05750	89373
25	31606	64782	34027	56734	09365	20008	93559	78384
26	10452	33074	76718	99556	16026	00013	78411	95107
27	37016	64633	67301	50949	91298	74968	73631	57397
28	66725	97865	25409	37498	00816	99262	14471	10232
29	07380	74438	82120	17890	40963	55757	13492	68294
30	71621	57688	58256	47702	74724	89419	08025	68519
31	03466	13263	23917	20417	11315	52805	33072	07723
32	12692	32931	97387	34822	53775	91674	76549	37635
33	52192	30941	44998	17833	94563	23062	95725	38463
34	56691	72529	66063	73570	86860	68125	40436	31303
35	74952	43041	58869	15677	78598	43520	97521	83428
36	18752	43693	32867	53017	22661	39610	03796	02622
37	61691	04944	43111	28325	82319	65589	66048	98498
38	49197	63948	38947	60207	70667	39843	60607	15328
39	19436	87291	71684	74859	76501	93456	95714	92518
40	39143	64893	14606	13543	09621	68301	69817	52140
41	82244	67549	76491	09761	74494	91307	64222	66592
42	55847	56155	42878	23708	97999	40131	52360	90390
43	94095	95970	07826	25991	37584	56966	68623	83454
44	11751	69469	25521	44097	07511	88976	30122	67542
45	69902	08995	27821	11758	64989	61902	32121	28165
46	21850	25352	25556	92161	23592	43294	10479	37879
47	75850	46992	25165	55906	62339	88958	91717	15756
48	29648	22086	42581	85677	20251	39641	65786	80689
49	82740	28443	42734	25518	82827	35825	90288	32911
50	36842	42092	52075	83926	42875	71500	69216	01350

Source: Table of 105,000 Random Decimal Digits, Interstate Commerce Commission, 1949.